DISCOVERING

Four
Accounts
of the Good News

MARGARET NUTTING RALPH

First Volume of the New Testament
in the Series
DISCOVERING THE LIVING WORD

PAULIST PRESS
New York/Mahwah

Library of Congress Cataloging-in-Publication Data

Ralph, Margaret Nutting.
    Discovering the Gospels: four accounts of the good news/by
Margaret Nutting Ralph.
        p.   cm.
    Includes index.
    ISBN 0-8091-3200-1
    1. Bible.   N.T.   Gospels—Criticism, interpretation, etc.
2. Bible.   N.T.   Gospels—Study.   I. Title.
BS2555.2.R24   1990
226'.06—dc20   90-44148
                                                         CIP

Published by Paulist Press
997 Macarthur Boulevard
Mahwah, New Jersey 07430

Printed and bound in the
United States of America

Contents

The Gospel According to Luke

The Gospel According to John

To my son, Tony,
without whose help
I could never have written
this dedication.

Preface

Let me ask you a question. Can you think of any book with a story line that you would expect to understand if you read only random paragraphs once a week?

"Of course not," you might respond. "What a ridiculous suggestion."

However, isn't that just what many of us do with the books in the Bible? We hear one paragraph from here, another from there on various Sundays. But few of us ever sit down and read one book in the Bible from beginning to end the way we would a novel.

As a result few of us have a clear picture of any one book. We would not be able to begin to compare, for instance, one gospel to another. If asked "Why did Luke write a gospel since he already had Mark's?" we would be completely in the dark. "Luke had Mark? You mean Luke wanted to say something Mark didn't?"

The premise behind this book on the gospels is that one will understand each gospel much better if one begins by reading the gospel.

Without stopping to read footnotes, hear lectures, or look up puzzling passages in a commentary, students should read the gospel through quickly the way one would a novel. As the students read they should keep paper and pen handy. Whenever the students come across a passage that is puzzling they should jot down the chapter and verse as well as the question which has come to mind. Rather than stop to seek the answer then, they should read on.

After the students have read an entire gospel they will have a completely different perspective from which to tackle their questions. Questions will no longer be isolated questions but questions in context. They will no longer be someone else's questions but their own. Students may notice that their questions are related to each other so that a single insight solves a number of difficulties. They may discover that they have brought a presumption to the gospel which is inaccurate and this presumption blocks them from understanding what they have read. After all, we do not come to the text fresh as Mark's original audience would have come to his little volume. Rather, we come with a variety of understandings, and perhaps misunderstandings, which we have learned somewhere else and have unconsciously projected onto the text.

Over the years I have collected the questions which seem to consistently come to the minds of thoughtful and curious students as they read the gospels of Mark, Matthew, Luke and John. The short articles which follow are responses to these questions which students have asked.

It is my experience that the content of these articles is appropriate and useful for juniors in high school and anyone older. I do not recommend this book for most younger students. I have found that one must have developed beyond the very "literal" way of thinking which is normal in the early teen years before one is able to understand the points made in these articles.

The quantity of material is appropriate for a variety of religious education settings. If two articles were discussed every class meeting, this book would be a one quarter course for an in school class that meets every day, a semester course for an in school class that meets two to three times a week, and a year long course for an out of school class that meets once a week. One may, of course, go faster or slower, depending on how much time is spent on the review and discussion questions. The material is also appropriate for adult education groups.

The format of question and response may tempt the students to skip responses to questions which have not occurred to them. This would be a mistake. One question often leads to related questions which do not appear in the heading but which are addressed in the articles.

Despite the question and answer format the short articles written in response to specific questions are not pat answers. I have tried to respond to the questions in such a way as to teach a methodology, so as to enable students to think. The goal is to equip students with the tools which they will need to search out answers to questions which do not appear in these articles.

The fact that the responses deal with methodology is an additional reason to read the articles in order. Methodological points made in early articles are usually not repeated in subsequent articles.

It may be that a student will be unfamiliar with a word or concept in a given article which has been presumed known and so is not explained. The glossary in the back of the book has been designed to help the student in such a situation. Students should remember to use the glossary if unfamiliar words appear or to review concepts which were explained in earlier articles.

Both teachers and students may expect, and even want, to read more introductory material before reading the gospel. This desire is purposefully thwarted in this book in an attempt to let the gospels themselves have the first word. Some background information is provided in various articles as the need arises. However, the student is urged to read the gospels first and to let the gospels speak for themselves. In this way questions are not explained away before the student has had an opportunity to ask them. All commentary is secondary to actually reading the gospels.

The background material given in the articles does not deal with what are really non-essential discussions giving the pros and cons for particular authors or geographic settings. Some additional information on these topics can be found in the glossary under the topic "authors," under the listing for each gospel, and under the name of each person to whom a gospel has been attributed.

In addition to a glossary, the book contains an index of biblical references. This will help both teacher and student to locate comments on given passages.

Some questions would naturally come to mind in more than one gospel. Questions which students have about Mark's gospel which are not addressed may reoccur in Matthew's or Luke's gospel and so be discussed in later articles. This is not to say that passages which appear in more than one gospel are identical. They may be in different contexts entirely. But what is said about a passage in the context of one gospel may well shed light on the passage as it appears in another gospel.

Of course not all questions which students raise will be addressed in this book. This is all to the good. To grow in one's ability to raise the questions, to explore answers and to live with mystery are goals in themselves. While it is wonderful to reach a degree of understanding as we read the gospels, not one of us will ever succeed in completely understanding the truth and wisdom which are to be found in the gospels of Mark, Matthew, Luke and John.

THE GOSPEL ACCORDING
to Mark

ARTICLE 1

Mark's Gospel Not History
or Biography

Question: "Why is there nothing in Mark's gospel about Jesus' life before his baptism?"

This question immediately makes it clear that we come to Mark's gospel with expectations which we impose on the gospel instead of simply reading this gospel and discovering what it is by reading it. Had we never read stories about Jesus' birth in Matthew's and Luke's gospels we would not ask this question because we would not expect a birth narrative. We would let Mark begin where Mark wants to begin.

However, the question will enable us to give a little background information which will not only make Mark's gospel more understandable but Matthew's and Luke's as well.

The fact that one expects a birth narrative is evidence that one may presume two facts, neither of which is accurate.

The first presumption is that the gospels should all be alike. If Matthew and Luke have stories of Jesus' birth so should Mark.

The gospels are not just alike. Each gospel is written in a unique social setting to meet the needs of a particular audience. To understand the gospel one must take into account the dialogue which is taking place between Mark and his audience of persecuted Christians, probably in Rome, who lived a full generation after Jesus, around 65 A.D.

Of the four gospels which appear in the New Testament, Mark's was written first. Even though Mark precedes Matthew and Luke, we should not picture Mark as an eyewitness passing on a first-hand eyewitness account of the events of Jesus' life.

THE GOSPEL ACCORDING TO MARK

DATE	65 A.D.
AUDIENCE	Persecuted Christians
SOURCES	The inherited oral and written traditions of the believing community
ORGANIZATION	The passion, death, and resurrection preceded by some miracle stories and some controversies with the Pharisees.
THEME	"Why should anyone suffer?" Look to Christ and see that suffering leads to resurrection.
GOES BACK TO . . .	The baptism of Jesus

This brings us to the second false presumption which might lie behind the question, "Why did Mark not include a birth narrative?" Mark is not writing a history book about the events of Jesus' life. Nor is he writing a biography. Rather Mark is writing a gospel.

The word "gospel" means "good news." Mark is writing good news to an audience that is in desperate need of it.

Mark's goal is not to give a complete account of Jesus' life. Rather he is selecting details from what he knows about Jesus' life. He is selecting details from the inherited oral and written traditions about Jesus which have grown up in the believing community. Of these many traditions Mark selects those which will be useful to him in passing on the good news which his audience needs to hear.

Mark's audience is having to choose between fidelity to their newly embraced "Christianity" and death. Will they deny Jesus and save their lives? Or will they affirm their belief in the risen Christ and be eaten by a lion in the Coliseum? Could death be the end of their story?

Mark is writing his gospel to help people have the strength to choose death because death is not death. Just look at Jesus. Jesus didn't want to die. He too would have liked to have avoided the suffering which his vocation involved. However, Jesus was faithful and look what happened. Death led to life. This is good news indeed.

Jesus' early years were not of great interest to Mark or his audience. It is only in later gospels that any interest in Jesus' early life or in his family seems to have developed.

Review Questions

1. Does Mark present himself as a first-hand eyewitness of the events of Jesus' life? On what in Mark's gospel do you base your answer?
2. Should we read Mark's gospel with the same frame of mind with which we read a history book? Why or why not?
3. Who is Mark's audience? To what question do they need an answer?

Discussion Questions

1. Do you think of the gospel as "good news"? Has the gospel "good news" helped you in time of trouble? When? How?
2. Do you have more faith in the account of a single eyewitness or in an account which has grown out of the experience of a community? Why?
3. Are you aware of other expectations you personally had when you read Mark which didn't turn out to be appropriate? What are they? Do you know why you had them?

ARTICLE 2

Stories Had Different Functions

Question: "Wasn't it imprudent to follow Jesus without knowing him? Wasn't it wrong for James and John to leave their father Zebedee in the boat? After all, we're supposed to honor our father and mother." (Mark 1:16–20; Mark 1:29 also discussed)

Once again these questions reveal a presumption, an expectation, a frame of mind that is going to get in the way of a person who wants to understand the gospels. The presumption behind the question is that Mark is trying to tell the story of the call of the apostles with the kind of realism with which a journalist or an historian would describe events. This is inaccurate.

The inherited oral and written traditions which Mark used to compile his good news were individual units of material which had grown up in the believing community to fulfill a variety of functions. Some material grew up as evangelizers preached the good news to those who had not yet heard it. Stories about the end of Jesus' life, about his passion, death and resurrection, as well as miracle stories would fall into this "evangelizing" category.

Stories about what Jesus said would be used in a different setting. They would be used when a community who already believed would come together. Such a believing community would want to understand what ramifications all that had happened should have on their choices, on their relationships. They would need to know and discuss what Jesus had said.

Creeds and rituals also began to develop within the worshiping community. These had a different function than did accounts of Jesus' sayings.

So by the time Mark was collating his material in 65 A.D. the

---

ORDER OF DEVELOPMENT
OF GOSPEL MATERIALS

- Accounts of the passion, death, and resurrection
- Miracle stories
- Sayings
- Birth narratives

---

materials from which he was choosing had taken on various forms and functions.

The story of the call of the disciples seems to have been formed to illustrate the wholehearted response that is necessary in order to follow Christ. Through stories such as this, early Christians would be taught that a relationship with Christ is no casual relationship that is simply added to life as it has always been lived. Rather, a "yes" to Christ is a radical conversion which will become central to all of one's choices and all of one's relationships.

In other words, such stories are a mixture of a core historical event and a story told with a certain emphasis to illustrate a point.

It seems evident that the gospel editors did not intend us to read the story as a completely literal account of events. If they had we would not immediately see Jesus at the home of Peter's mother-in-law (Mark 1:29).

In order to understand the gospels we must learn what kind of writing we are reading. We must understand the literary form of each gospel (we should not presume they are all the same), and even the literary form of individual stories within a gospel. If we do not take into account the literary form we will misunderstand the intent of the author and we will misunderstand the revelation which that author hopes to pass on through his writing.

Review Questions

1. What kinds of oral and written traditions had grown up in the early church by the time Mark was writing?
2. How did function (what the person who was speaking was trying to accomplish) affect form (the way the story was molded)?
3. What point about belief in Jesus Christ is illustrated by the story of the call of the apostles?

Discussion Questions

1. Do you understand what we mean when we say that Mark is not writing as a journalist or an historian would? Explain.
2. What is involved in conversion? Do you think really believing in Jesus Christ changes your choices and your relationships? How?

ARTICLE 3

Mark's Dramatic Irony

Question: "Why were all the people amazed when Jesus cast the unclean spirit out of the man? Wouldn't they expect the Son of God to be able to do these things?" (Mark 1:27; Mark 4:40 also discussed)

This question is related to many questions which students have about the reaction of both the crowds and the apostles to Jesus. After reading Mark's account of the calming of the storm (Mark 4:40) students inquire, "Why do the apostles ask, 'Who is this?' Don't they know?"

Again these questions arise from our tendency to project onto the gospel some impressions which we already have but for which there is no evidence in the text.

In this case the presumption is that the crowd or the apostles understand that Jesus was divine during the time he was teaching and healing, and before his passion, death and resurrection. Mark gives us no reason to think that Jesus' contemporaries were able to grasp the significance of his identity and his mission until after the resurrection.

As Mark writes his gospel both he and his audience understand that Jesus was divine. They have post-resurrection insight. Because Jesus rose from the dead and because the believing community has experienced the power and presence of the risen Christ they have come to understand who Jesus actually was. So Mark can begin his story with the words, "The beginning of the gospel of Jesus Christ, the Son of God" (Mark 1:1).

However, in doing this Mark sets up a situation between his readers and his text which is called dramatic irony.

Dramatic irony exists when the readers know something which the characters in the story do not know. The characters in the story slowly grow to understand what the reading audience has known all along.

This is exactly the way Mark writes his gospel. He and the audience know that Jesus is the Son of God. However, the crowd and the apostles do not. We are then confronted with some amazing phenomena—healings and exorcisms among them. We see the crowds and the apostles struggling to understand what all this means. However, to think that they should immediately jump to the conclusion that Jesus is the Son of God is to misunderstand their situation entirely.

For one thing, no one was expecting God to become man. (We will talk more about what the Jews were expecting in a "messiah" shortly.) For another, miracle workers were not uncommon. Jesus would not be the only person about whom they had heard who would be categorized as a "miracle worker." Jesus' contemporaries were confronted with a profound mystery, one upon which little light was cast until after the resurrection.

We will find the events and interactions in Mark's gospel much easier to understand if we can refrain from assuming that Jesus' contemporaries had Mark's or our post-resurrection point of view.

Review Questions

1. What is dramatic irony? In what way does Mark's gospel illustrate dramatic irony?
2. Did Jesus' miracles prove to his contemporaries that he was divine? Why or why not?
3. When did Jesus' contemporaries finally understand that Jesus was divine?

Discussion Questions

1. Have you personally heard about or talked to someone who claimed a miraculous healing? What is your reaction to such stories? Why?

2. Had you been present when Jesus healed someone, how do you think you would have reacted? Can you think of some possible explanations other than that the person is God become man? What are some other explanations?

ARTICLE 4

"Miracles": A Form of Preaching

Question: "Why did Jesus so often tell people to be quiet after he healed them? You'd think that he would want them to tell everyone so more people would believe in him." (Mark 1:43; 5:43; 7:36; Mark 1:15; 1:45; 1:38; 3:9; 5:19 also discussed)

This question reflects a presumption that Jesus worked miracles in order to help people figure out who he is.

The question "Who is Jesus?" is certainly central to Mark's gospel and Mark's theme. However, we cannot presume that the focus which Mark has when he passes on the good news to his persecuted audience is identical to the focus which Jesus had when he preached to his audience.

Jesus' focus seems to have been not so much "Who am I?" as "The kingdom of God is at hand." In fact Mark pictures Jesus' first words as being: "The time is fulfilled, and the kingdom of God is at hand; repent, and believe the gospel" (Mark 1:15).

Jesus' miracles are another way of preaching the kingdom. God's power is breaking in upon his people and freeing them from whatever has held them in bondage.

However, the healings cause Jesus some problems. Like us, Jesus' contemporaries often seem to be more interested in their physical well-being than in their spiritual well-being. The more people know of Jesus' healings, the more difficult it becomes for him to preach the good news of the kingdom.

Why? Because the crowds constantly press upon Jesus for healing. When Jesus told the leper not to tell anyone, the leper immediately told everyone so that "Jesus could no longer openly

---

**SOME PASSAGES IN MARK'S GOSPEL IN WHICH
JESUS WARNS, "DO NOT TELL."**

After a healing

1:43
5:43
7:36
(However, in 5:19 Jesus says "do tell.")

After self-revelation to the apostles

8:30
9:9

After evil spirits have named him

1:25
3:12

---

enter a town, but was out in the country, and people came to him from every quarter" (Mark 1:45).

It became necessary for Jesus to avoid the crowd in order to accomplish his purposes. Early on when the crowd, who knew of his healings, were looking for him, Jesus told Simon, "Let us go on to the next towns, that I may preach there also; for that is why I came out" (Mark 1:38).

The crowds not only made it hard for Jesus to preach. They also made it hard for him to pray, to teach his disciples, even to eat. In fact, the crowd was sometimes a danger. The reason Jesus occasionally taught from a boat was that there was danger he would be crushed by those wanting to be healed (see Mark 3:9).

So it is quite understandable that Jesus would ask those whom he healed not to excite the crowds.

One notable exception to this pattern of asking people not to tell is in the account of the cure of the Gerasene demoniac who wants to go with Jesus. Jesus tells him: "Go home to your friends and tell them how much the Lord has done for you" (Mark 5:19). In this instance the people, far from swamping Jesus, are afraid of him and are asking him to leave.

However, the story of the Gerasene demoniac has many puzzling features which we will be discussing later. There is a question as to whether or not we should interpret this account as a literal account of events.

In any event Jesus had good reason to ask people to be quiet about his healing. Otherwise the healings might have become an end in themselves rather than an integral part of Jesus' preaching about the coming of the kingdom.

Review Questions

1. Why did Jesus work miracles?
2. Why did Mark repeat stories about Jesus' miracles?
3. Why did Jesus tell people to be quiet about his miracles?

Discussion Questions

1. Do you think you are more interested in your physical health or in your spiritual health? What behaviors reveal your priorities? Are the two connected in any way? How?
2. Have you ever had to "hide from the crowd" in order to accomplish what you needed to accomplish? When?
3. Are you surprised to discover that Jesus did not always respond to the demands that others placed on him? Why or why not? Do you always respond to the demands of others? Should you? Why or why not?

ARTICLE 5

Mark Emphasizes Jesus' Humanity

Question: "Why would Jesus have to pray? After all, Jesus is God." (Mark 1:35; 6:46; 14:32; 14:35; 14:39; Mark 4:40; 5:30; 6:5; 8:15–18; 11:12–14; 13:32; 14:15 also discussed)

Many students who read the gospel for the first time bring with them a much clearer idea of Jesus Christ as God than they do of Jesus Christ as a human being. For such a person the gospel of Mark is very puzzling. Mark seems to emphasize the humanity of Jesus.

Not only does Jesus seem to need to pray, but he admits that he doesn't know everything when he says that only the Father knows when "all these things will take place" (Mark 13:32).

As Mark tells the story it seems that Jesus does not always have control over his own healing power. When the woman with the flow of blood is healed by touching the hem of Jesus' garment, Mark tells us that Jesus, "perceiving in himself that power had gone forth from him, immediately turned about in the crowd and said, 'Who touched my garments?' " (Mark 5:30).

In addition, Mark says that Jesus "could do no mighty work" in his hometown because the people did not have faith in him (Mark 6:5).

Not only does Jesus seem to lack control over his healing power in Mark's gospel, but he also seems to lack control over his own emotions. Jesus is very often angry and impatient with the disciples. After the calming of the storm he asks, "Why are you afraid? Have you no faith?" (Mark 4:40).

Jesus is simply fed up with the disciples after the second miracle of the loaves when they get on a boat to leave. Jesus is worried

19

JESUS PRAYS

In Mark's Gospel
1:35
6:46
14:32
14:35
14:39

In Matthew's Gospel
14:23
19:13
26:36
26:39
26:42
26:44

In Luke's Gospel
3:21
5:16
6:12
9:18
9:28
9:29
11:1
22:41
22:44
22:45

---

about the bad effect which the Pharisees are capable of having on others. So he warns the disciples to "take heed, beware of the leaven of the Pharisees and the leaven of Herod" (Mark 8:15). The disciples are concerned about having enough bread. They misunderstand the metaphor of "leaven" and say, "We have no bread."

Jesus seems to be furious. He responds with anger and impatience. "Why do you discuss the fact that you have no bread? Do you not yet perceive or understand? Are your hearts hardened? Having eyes, do you not see, and having ears, do you not hear?" (Mark 8:17–18).

However, of all the pictures which we get of Jesus in Mark's gospel none reveals Jesus' humanness more than the cursing of the fig tree. Jesus was hungry, "and seeing in the distance a fig tree in leaf, he went to see if he could find anything on it. When he came to it, he found nothing but leaves, for it was not the season for figs. And he said to it, 'May no one ever eat fruit from you again' " (Mark 11:12–14).

Why would Jesus act so unreasonably? And why would Mark picture Jesus acting like this?

Perhaps the answer to why Mark seems to emphasize Jesus' humanity lies with the particular audience to whom Mark is speaking. Mark's audience is facing the same kind of excruciatingly painful and premature death which Jesus himself faced. They know what it is like to be angry and exasperated. They know what it is like to face temptation. They know what it is like to pray in agony that "if it were possible the hour might pass" from them (Mark 14:15).

Mark wants his audience to understand that martyrdom was not easy for Jesus either. He suffered just as they are suffering. However, despite his anger, his exasperation, his dread of what he must endure, Jesus remained faithful and passed through death to life. Mark wants to give his audience the courage to do the same. He hopes they will find that courage by keeping their eyes on Jesus, who understands all their needs.

"Why did Jesus have to pray?" Because Jesus experienced life as human beings do. Jesus, like us, needed to seek out God's will in prayer.

Review Questions

1. What are some of the passages in which Mark emphasizes the humanity of Jesus?
2. Why would Mark choose to show Jesus as a person who was not always "in perfect control"?

3. What did Mark hope his audience would gain from this picture of Jesus?

Discussion Questions

1. Do you think it possible that Jesus couldn't work a miracle because of others' lack of faith? Why or why not?
2. Have you ever felt so angry that you thought you might lose control? Do you picture God as disapproving of such a feeling? Why or why not?
3. Have you ever displaced your anger from a person to a thing as Jesus did with the fig tree? Is this kind of displacement "healthy" psychologically?

ARTICLE 6

The "Son of Man" Will Suffer

Question: "Why did Jesus call himself the Son of Man since he was really the Son of God? Wouldn't this mislead people?" (Mark 2:10; 2:28; 8:31; see chart for complete listing of "Son of Man" passages; Daniel 7:9–10, 13–14; Mark 13:24–26 also discussed)

In an earlier article we mentioned that while Mark is definitely centering in on the question "Who is Jesus?" Jesus himself seemed to emphasize more the imminent coming of the kingdom.

However, Jesus is pictured in Mark's gospel as applying a messianic title to himself, and that title is "Son of Man." In fact "Son of Man" is the only messianic title which we find on Jesus' lips in Mark's gospel.

What is a messianic title? It is a title which identifies a person as the expected messiah. Some other messianic titles are "messiah" and "Christ," both of which mean "the anointed one," and "Son of David" which reflects the belief that the messiah would be someone in David's line.

In order to understand why Jesus is pictured as referring to himself as "Son of Man" we must ask ourselves what those words would have meant to the audience to whom Jesus spoke.

When the apostles heard the phrase "Son of Man" they would have been reminded of the book of Daniel in the Old Testament. In this apocalyptic book, written to offer hope to the Jews who were suffering persecution at the hands of Antiochus Epiphanes (167–164 B.C.), the author uses the phrase "Son of Man" to refer to the hoped-for messiah.

PASSAGES IN MARK IN WHICH JESUS IS CALLED "SON OF MAN"

2:10	10:33
2:28	10:45
8:31	13:36
8:38	14:21
9:9	14:41
9:12	14:62
9:31	

In chapter 7 of the book of Daniel the author describes a vision of heaven.

> Thrones were set in place and one of great age took his seat. His robe was white as snow, the hair of his head as pure as wool. His throne was a blaze of flames, its wheels were a burning fire. A stream of fire poured out issuing from his presence. A thousand thousand waited on him, ten thousand times ten thousand stood before him. A court was held and the books were opened (Daniel 7:9–10).

The vision continues:

> I gazed into the vision of the night. And I saw, coming on the clouds of heaven, one like a son of man. He came to the one of great age and was led into his presence. On him was conferred sovereignty, glory and kingship, and men of all peoples, nations and languages became his servants. His sovereignty is an eternal sovereignty which shall never pass away, nor will his empire ever be destroyed (Daniel 7:13–14).

In Mark's gospel Jesus is shown using this same apocalyptic image of the messiah.

> But in those days, after that time of distress, the sun will be darkened, the moon will lose its brightness, the stars will come falling from heaven and the powers in the heavens will

be shaken. And then they will see the Son of Man coming on the clouds with great power and glory (Mark 13:24–26).

So to Jesus' audience the words "Son of Man" would refer to this great and glorious messiah. However, when Jesus applies the image to himself he tries to make it clear that this great and glorious messiah must first suffer.

And he began to teach them that the Son of Man was destined to suffer grievously, to be rejected by the elders and the chief priests and the scribes, and to be put to death, and after three days to rise again (Mark 8:31).

The apostles just couldn't grasp this idea. They were not expecting a suffering messiah.

Mark emphasizes that the "Son of Man" must suffer because this idea is at the core of Mark's message to his audience of persecuted Christians. He does not want them to forget that the glorious "Son of Man's" victory was reached through the cross. Death would not be a defeat for them any more than it had been for the "Son of Man."

Review Questions

1. To what would the phrase "Son of Man" refer in the minds of Jesus' audience?
2. What concept did Jesus try to add to his followers' understanding of the "Son of Man"?
3. Why would Mark emphasize a suffering messiah for his audience?

Discussion Questions

1. Have you ever expected something or someone and later discovered that the reality was very different from your expectations? Explain. How does this relate to the apostles' experience of Jesus?

2. Have you ever tried to explain something about yourself to someone else and have him or her completely misunderstand? How did you feel? How does this experience relate to Jesus' experience in Mark's gospel?

3. Imagine you are visiting someone on death row. What about the good news of the gospel might you say to him or her? Would you say the same thing you would say to a new father or mother? How does this question relate to Mark's gospel?

ARTICLE 7

Jesus Speaks Ironically

Question: "Why did Jesus call the Pharisees 'righteous' when they weren't (Mark 2:17)? Is anyone so 'righteous' that he or she doesn't need to be saved?" (Mark 8:11–12 also discussed)

When Jesus refers to the Pharisees as "righteous" or "virtuous" in the context of Mark's gospel, we know that he is speaking ironically. The Pharisees are far from righteous. They are legalistic, judgmental, and hypocritical.

It is important to realize that Jesus sometimes uses irony when he speaks. A person speaks ironically when the literal meaning of that person's words is not identical to the intended meaning.

When you hear a person speak you can usually recognize irony by the tone. If you are reading a conversation rather than hearing it, irony must be determined by the context.

Jesus uses irony with the Pharisees on several occasions. The case in point, when he refers to them as "righteous" just when they are fingering others as sinners and are unable to see their own sinfulness, is a case in point.

Another example of Jesus' use of irony with the Pharisees comes when the Pharisees ask Jesus for a sign (Mark 8:11–12). Mark says, "And he sighed deeply in his spirit, and said, 'Why does this generation seek a sign? Truly, I say to you, no sign shall be given to this generation' " (Mark 8:12).

Obviously these words are ironic. Of all the generations on the face of the earth Jesus' generation received the greatest signs both in his ministry and in his resurrection.

Why does Jesus use irony? In this conversation with the Pharisees we get the sense that Jesus is exasperated. The Pharisees ask for a sign, not so that they may believe but to test Jesus. Mark places this acrimonious encounter right after the second multiplication of the loaves. Obviously signs have been available. Mark has Jesus show us his exasperation by saying that Jesus sighed deeply.

Then Jesus exaggerates. He doesn't say, "No sign will be given to you Pharisees." Rather he says, "No sign will be given to this generation." Since this statement is literally not true, we know that Jesus' tone must be ironic. Translated, Jesus' words mean, "How can you ask for a sign? I'm giving you constant signs."

Jesus uses irony quite often when he speaks, not just with the Pharisees but with the apostles and crowds too. Usually Jesus uses irony when he is exasperated, when he is trying to teach something and is being met with open hostility, or when he is being met with someone's total inability to understand.

The Pharisees are just plain blind to their own faults. When Jesus says he didn't come for the "righteous but for sinners," he is ironically pointing out that the Pharisees are among the sinners for whom he has come. He is not saying that some people do not need him.

Review Questions

1. Are the Pharisees virtuous? Why or why not?
2. Does Jesus refuse to give the Pharisees a sign? Explain.
3. What is irony? If you are reading rather than hearing a conversation, how can you recognize irony?

Discussion Questions

1. Do you use irony in normal everyday conversation? Why might you use irony rather than saying exactly what you mean?

2. Do you see any difference between irony and sarcasm? Explain.
3. Have you ever tried to persuade someone to a point of view to which that person's mind was completely closed? How did you feel? How does this relate to Jesus' experience?

ARTICLE 8

Old Wineskins: Closed Minds

Question: "What in the world does Jesus mean when he starts talking about putting new patches on old garments and new wine into old wineskins (Mark 2:21–22)? Is all of this somehow related to the question about fasting?" (Mark 2:23; 3:1–6; 7:1–8 also discussed)

Yes, all of this is related to the question of fasting, in a way. It is important to remember that Jesus was a very different kind of religious leader than his audience had experienced before.

Jesus' contemporaries had a clear idea of what any good religious leader would be like, much more what the expected messiah would be like. Such a leader would be expected to fast, to refrain from any work on the sabbath, to perform ritual washings before eating—in sum, to obey the laws which prescribed many religious practices.

Jesus' behavior failed to match these expectations on many occasions. Jesus picked corn on the sabbath (Mark 2:23), healed on the sabbath (Mark 3:1–6), and defended his disciples when they ate without washing their hands (Mark 7:1–8).

All of this behavior made the Pharisees dislike Jesus. Since they had already defined in their minds how a good person would act they were unable to recognize that Jesus was a good person when he failed to conform to their expectations.

It is this frame of mind that Jesus is speaking about in his analogies of the patch and the new wineskin. He is trying to tell the Pharisees that their mental categories are not going to work in relation to him. Jesus and his teachings will tear apart, burst the seams of the Pharisees' tight little categories.

To warn the Pharisees that they are failing to understand the significance of his presence in their midst and of their own time in history, he asks, "Can the wedding guests fast while the bridegroom is with them?" Jesus is telling the Pharisees that theirs is a unique time in history, different from the times of the ancestors. It is a time when obedience to all the old rules will not suffice if such obedience gives one a sense of complacency, a sense that one is doing all that is required. Instead of opening up the Pharisees' minds to mystery and truth, such practices are giving the Pharisees the false sense that they already know everything and have no reason to reassess, to be open to new insights.

So the Pharisees' frame of mind is like an old cloth or like an old wineskin. It can't accommodate anything new. Their closed minds are as unable to accommodate Jesus' new truth as an old cloth is unable to support a new patch or an old wineskin is unable to hold new wine. To understand Jesus the Pharisees will need to have a conversion of mind. New wine calls for new wineskins.

Jesus' early warning to the Pharisees, that they would not be able to comprehend him and his truths with their narrow mental categories, turns out to be exactly right. The Pharisees find Jesus' challenge to their legalistic and self-righteous attitudes so threatening that they want to get rid of him.

Review Questions

1. What were the Pharisees expecting in a religious leader?
2. In what ways did Jesus fail to meet these expectations?
3. What is Jesus telling the Pharisees about themselves in his analogies of the new patch and the new wineskin?

Discussion Questions

1. Do you think religious rules and practices have a place in the church? What place?

2. Do you think obeying rules can ever be the essential ingredient of a holy life? Why or why not?
3. Is there any idea which you have heard recently which made you feel frightened or defensive about your beliefs? What was it? What do you think would be the best response for you to have when this happens? Why?

ARTICLE 9

Jesus' "Socratic" Irony

Question: "Isn't Jesus sometimes mean and unresponsive to the Pharisees and scribes? He baits them when he cures the man with the withered hand (Mark 3:1–6) and he refuses to tell them that his authority is from God (Mark 11:27–33). No wonder they don't realize who Jesus is."

Jesus has a real problem on his hands when it comes to the Pharisees. They are predisposed to think ill of Jesus. He cannot be true to his vocation, to his sense of who he is and what he is to say and do, without aggravating, challenging and criticizing the Pharisees.

To Jesus there is a basic issue at stake. Should the law be observed to the point that one is forbidden to act lovingly toward one's neighbor, to do what is obviously for the other's good? The Pharisees act as though they think it should.

In the scene where Jesus cures the man with the withered hand we see the Pharisees predisposed to criticize Jesus for disobeying a law even though it is obviously for the good of the man that his withered hand be healed.

Jesus puts the question to them bluntly. "Is it lawful on the sabbath to do good or to do harm, to save life or to kill?" (Mark 3:4). The word "lawful" is dripping with irony. In fact, the whole question is ironic.

A question such as this is an example of what is called Socratic irony. Socrates taught by asking questions. The questions seemed simple-minded and off the subject. However, they were neither. The questions were asked not to inform the questioner but to inform the one to whom the question was addressed.

In this case Jesus seems to think the question is about the "sabbath law." Actually Jesus knows the question is much bigger than that. The question is really, "How is one to love a neighbor?" But he couches the question as though it were about the sabbath law because that is what the Pharisees are thinking.

By wording the question the way he does Jesus hopes that the Pharisees will see that the law is not meant to forbid acts of love and kindness. Of course not. But the Pharisees remain silent. They are hard-hearted.

The same sort of acrimonious interaction is taking place when the scribes ask Jesus who gave him his authority. Jesus asks a Socratic question: "Was the baptism of John from heaven or from men?" The question appears to be off the subject. However, in responding to the question the scribes learn something about themselves. They learn that they are unwilling to tell the truth as they understand it ("All held that John was a real prophet") and they lie about their unwillingness. They answer, "We do not know." Of course they do know, but they won't say.

Jesus is aware that they are lying and aware that they themselves realize they are lying, so Jesus says, "Neither will I tell you by what authority I do these things" (Mark 11:33). The words "Neither will I tell you" calls them on their lie. However, the remark is ironic because Jesus, by his original question, has told the Pharisees from whom his authority comes. Both his authority and John's come from God.

Jesus is not baiting the Pharisees nor being unresponsive to them. He is simply pursuing his vocation as teacher of the truth, and dealing with a closed-minded and antagonistic audience as best he can.

Review Questions

1. What is a Socratic question?
2. In his conversation with the Pharisees when Jesus cures the man with the withered hand, why does he frame the question as though it were a question of sabbath law?

3. Does Jesus fail to tell the Pharisees where he gets his authority?

Discussion Questions

1. Have you ever had a teacher who asked Socratic questions? Was the teacher good? Why or why not?
2. Do you think asking questions is an effective way to teach? Why or why not?
3. Have you ever had a closed mind in regard to someone who was speaking to you? When? Do you know any way that person could have reached you? How?

ARTICLE 10

Forgiveness Not Always Received

Question: "Why is blasphemy against the Holy Spirit an unforgivable sin (Mark 3:29)? I thought there was no such thing as an unforgivable sin." (Mark 3:22–27 also discussed)

In order to respond to this question we will have to break it down into two parts. "What is this sin that Jesus calls 'blasphemy against the Holy Spirit'?" And, secondly, "Why is this sin unforgivable?"

In order to understand the kind of sin to which Jesus is referring we must put his words into context. Jesus' words are the conclusion to the following account:

> The scribes who had come down from Jerusalem said, "He is possessed by Beelzebul, and by the prince of demons he casts out demons." And he called them to him, and said to them in parables, "How can Satan cast out Satan? If a kingdom is divided against itself, that kingdom cannot stand. And if a house is divided against itself, that house will not be able to stand. And if Satan has run up against himself and is divided, he cannot stand, but is coming to an end. But no one can enter a strong man's house and plunder his goods, unless he first binds the strong man; then indeed he may plunder his house" (Mark 3:22–27).

It is as a conclusion to this conversation that Jesus remarks on the "unforgivable sin."

The context for Jesus' statement, then, is one in which the scribes are interpreting Jesus' mighty deeds not as signs of the inbreaking of the kingdom of God but as signs of an evil presence, as signs of Satan.

36

As we have already seen, the scribes have a constantly acrimonious relationship with Jesus. Mark has established a clear pattern in the scribes' reaction to Jesus. They have a strong predisposition to find fault. They want to believe the worst.

For this reason Jesus calls the scribes to him and makes a special attempt to reason with them. He points out that it makes no sense to attribute his power to Satan rather than to God because Satan would not be fighting himself. If Jesus is casting out demons he must not be a tool of Satan. He must have power over Satan.

Then Jesus makes the statement about the unforgivable sin. This comment is one example of several in which Jesus simply remarks on the order of things. He knows he has made no headway with the scribes.

Jesus is dealing with a group of people who are predisposed to find fault and think the worst of him. As a result of this predisposition they see what is of God and label it evil. It is this refusal to recognize what is of God that Jesus refers to as "blasphemy against the Holy Spirit."

A person who refuses to recognize good will never have forgiveness precisely because he or she will never recognize the spiritual order, will never recognize his or her own faults, and so will fail to repent.

It is the lack of repentance which results in the person not having forgiveness—not lack of forgiveness offered, but lack of forgiveness received.

In the context of Mark's gospel Jesus' observation about the "eternal" nature of the sin which the scribes are committing turns out to be accurate. Jesus' relationship with the scribes continues to grow worse until the scribes finally send men with swords and clubs to do away with this "evil" Jesus. The scribes never do repent and so they never do have the forgiveness which Jesus longs to give them.

Review Questions

1. In the context of Mark's gospel what is the unforgivable sin?
2. Why is this an unforgivable sin?

3. Is Jesus' observation about "the way things are" accurate?
Explain.

Discussion Questions

1. Is there ever a time when Jesus does not invite repentance?
Explain.
2. What is the difference between forgiveness offered and forgiveness received?
3. Have you ever wanted to be reconciled with someone who
refused to be reconciled with you? What can you do under
such circumstances?

ARTICLE 11

Apocalyptic Literature

Question: "In the story of the Gerasene demoniac why did Jesus let the demons enter the pigs? Why did the pigs drown? Did Jesus pay the owner for the loss of his pigs?" (Mark 5:1–20)

The story of the exorcism of Legion from the Gerasene demoniac puzzles nearly everyone who reads it. In fact there are so many strange details in the story that scripture scholars suggest that the author is purposefully warning the reader that the real meaning of the story does not lie in its surface meaning.

Perhaps the story is not meant to be an account of an event at all. Perhaps it is an example of apocalyptic writing.

Apocalyptic writing is a kind of literature written in code to people suffering under persecution. Its purpose is always to build hope in those who are persecuted by assuring them that God will save them and defeat their enemies. The reason apocalyptic literature is always in code is so that only the persecuted people will understand it, not those who are doing the persecuting.

As was mentioned in an earlier article, Mark's audience is suffering from persecution. It would be perfectly appropriate for him to include an apocalyptic story in his gospel in order to assure his audience that God was going to save them. In order to understand the message in such a story one would have to interpret the symbols.

The key to the symbols used in the story is the recurring military terminology. The word "legion" refers to a division of Roman soldiers. A "herd of pigs" refers to a group of military recruits. (Real pigs don't travel in "herds.") "He gave them leave" is also military terminology.

> ### SOME CHARACTERISTICS OF
> ### APOCALYPTIC WRITING
>
> Audience: Persecuted people
> Method: Written in code
> Message: Have hope—God will save

That the pigs run into the sea is an allusion to the fate of the Egyptian army at the time of the exodus. The number of pigs who drown—two thousand—is the number of soldiers who make up a legion.

To Mark's audience, persecuted Christians, the story would have been a message in code telling them to maintain faith and hope. God would defeat the Romans who were persecuting them just as he had defeated the Egyptians.

What is one to make of such an interpretation? Could the story be apocalyptic literature? If this story does not have its roots in an event, does that mean that other New Testament accounts are not based on events either?

The core of the problem is one of literary form. To understand any story we must understand the form, because to misunderstand the form is to misunderstand the intent of the author.

In this case there is reason to look for a deeper meaning because the author signals his audience by referring to a "herd of pigs." To an audience who knows that pigs don't travel in herds this is a red flag. It has the same effect that a video-taped message from a prisoner of war would have if he mispronounced common words or got his wife's name wrong. He is really saying, "Don't take everything I say literally."

Is it possible that an isolated story is an example of apocalyptic writing and that the gospel as a whole is not? The answer to this is "yes." As was said before, the gospels are an edited arrangement of inherited oral and written traditions. They contain within them a variety of kinds of writing—parables, miracle stories, apocalyptic writings, infancy narratives, and more. Each type of story grew up independently. So it is fair to suggest that this story is an example of apocalyptic writing rather than an account of an exorcism.

Review Questions

1. What is apocalyptic literature?
2. What signal does the author give that we should look deeper than the literal meaning of his words to find his real meaning?
3. What is the key to the symbolism in this story?
4. What is the author saying to the audience through the symbols?

Discussion Questions

1. Does the literal level of the story of the Gerasene demoniac make sense to you? Why or why not?
2. Does it bother you to think that this story might not be an account of an event? Why or why not?
3. If this story is not about an event, does that mean that none of the miracle stories are about an event? Why or why not?

ARTICLE 12

Who Feeds the Hungry?

Question: "Why does Jesus tell the apostles to give the crowd something to eat themselves (Mark 6:34–41)? Isn't that asking the impossible?" (Mark 8:1–9 also discussed)

Jesus' words to the apostles, "You give them something to eat," seem strange if Jesus is planning to "multiply the loaves." Jesus' words put an emphasis in the story that seems incongruous with our understanding of what the story is all about.

At first reading the first multiplication of the loaves seems to be a story about Jesus working a miracle. It seems to be a straightforward account of an event. This impression is reinforced by those who have inserted "headings" in the English translations of Mark's gospel. This episode is sometimes preceded by the words, "First miracle of the loaves," or, "Jesus feeds the five thousand." These headings put the emphasis on Jesus as the one acting. Yet in the story itself Jesus puts the emphasis on the apostles acting. He says, "You give them to eat yourselves." Why?

It seems that the emphasis in the story is not on a miracle at all.

The apostles originally feel no responsibility for the people. They suggest that Jesus send the crowd away, "to go into the country and villages round about and buy themselves something to eat" (Mark 6:36).

Jesus suggests that they assume some responsibility. He requests simply that they share what they have.

The story then uses eucharistic imagery as it describes Jesus' actions in such a way that we connect the description here with the description of Jesus at the last supper. He "looked up to heaven, and blessed and broke the loaves, and gave them to the disciples" (Mark 6:41).

Rather than being a straightforward account of a miracle worked by Jesus, the story seems to be one which is teaching the church to take Jesus' words to the disciples to heart: "Give them to eat yourselves." If Mark's audience (or we as a society) all took those words to heart we would have enough resources to meet everyone's needs. That is what is meant by the twelve baskets of scraps. Twelve is a symbolic number representing the whole church (twelve tribes, twelve apostles). To say that twelve baskets are left is a way of saying that there is enough for everyone.

In Mark's gospel there is a second occasion on which a large crowd is fed (Mark 8:1–9). Again the disciples have no idea where food for so many might be found. Jesus' response is, "How many loaves have you?" Again the eucharistic imagery appears. This time the number of leftover baskets is seven, a number signifying wholeness or perfection.

In neither account of the feeding of the crowds does the text use the word "miracle" or "sign." Nor does the text describe a reaction of wonder on anyone's part. When the fact of a miracle is the emphasis in a story the response of the crowd to the mighty signs performed is an integral part of the story.

The question now becomes, "What is Mark teaching his audience through this story?" When Jesus says, "Give them to eat yourselves," the response of Mark's audience (and ours as well) is probably just like the disciples': "How can we do that?"

By using eucharistic imagery as he describes the blessing, and by picturing Jesus returning the bread to the disciples for distribution, Mark gives his audience and us an answer to the question.

Each of us can "give them to eat" because our power comes from the risen Christ who sent us his Spirit and with whom we join ourselves in the eucharist. Our efforts and his power, used to the full, would feed all.

Mark's message, therefore, is not so much, "God can work miracles," as it is, "You give them to eat, with Christ's help."

Review Questions

1. Does the account of the feeding of the multitude claim that Jesus is working a miracle? Why or why not?
2. What elements of the account put the emphasis on the disciples and their responsibility for the crowd?
3. What is this story teaching Mark's audience?

Discussion Questions

1. Do you feel resistant to the interpretation offered in this article? Why or why not?
2. Which is the more challenging message: "Jesus can work miracles," or "You give them to eat"? Why?
3. Do you understand what it means to say that the gospels include post-resurrection insight? How does this story illustrate such insight?

ARTICLE 13

"Miracles": Preaching or Proof?

Question: "You have suggested that the story of the exorcism of Legion into the pigs (Mark 5:1–20) and the two accounts of the feeding of the crowds (Mark 6:32–43; 8:1–9) are not told for the purpose of describing a miracle. Didn't Jesus work miracles? Aren't miracle stories usually about events?" (Mark 1:15; 2:11; 3:22 also discussed)

This question is one which pinpoints a core issue in understanding any part of the Bible, and one which comes up over and over: In order to understand any part of the Bible we must understand the kind of writing we are reading. To misunderstand the literary form is to misunderstand the intent of the author.

A gospel is an edited arrangement of a variety of different kinds of writing, different literary forms. One ramification of this fact is that what we say about one particular story in a gospel, we are not saying about the whole gospel.

To interpret the story of the exorcism of Legion into the pigs as apocalyptic literature (a coded message) is not to say, or even imply, that such an interpretation would be appropriate for the gospel as a whole or even for other miracle stories. To interpret the story of the feeding of the multitudes as one which teaches us to share what we have rather than one which emphasizes Jesus' role is not to say that this interpretation would be appropriate for the gospel as a whole. The stories must be treated individually.

"Did Jesus work miracles?" There seems to be no question that those who experienced Jesus experienced him as one who worked mighty signs, a "miracle worker." Even his enemies

45

recognized his power. But not all who experienced the power attributed it to God. As Mark tells us, some attributed Jesus' power to Satan (see Mark 3:22).

In other words, everyone agreed that Jesus had power, but the power didn't, in itself, prove anything. "Miracle workers" were common in the culture.

Then why did Jesus work miracles? As was explained in an earlier article, it appears that Jesus performed his mighty signs not so much to prove his identity as to proclaim his message: the imminent presence of the kingdom. Both signs and words were saying, "The kingdom of God is at hand. Repent, and believe in the gospel" (Mark 1:15).

While Jesus used his mighty signs to preach the good news of the kingdom, the early church used his mighty signs to preach the "gospel of Jesus Christ the Son of God" (Mark 1:1). In other words, Jesus did not preach himself, but the early church did preach Jesus Christ.

So the miracle stories are not answering the question, "What exactly happened?" Rather, they are answering the question, "What does what happened tell us about Jesus?"

In other words, the accounts which we call miracle stories have their roots in events, but the motive of the story teller is not to describe those events.

How does this change in emphasis change the way the story of a miracle is told?

In Mark's gospel the miracle stories are told in such a way that they emphasize Jesus' identity more than they emphasize the coming of the kingdom. For example, after healing a lame man Jesus is not pictured as saying, "The blind see again, the lame walk, lepers are cleansed, the deaf hear, the dead are raised to life, the good news is proclaimed to the poor," a statement which would have emphasized the breaking in of the kingdom. Rather Jesus is pictured as saying, "But that you may know that the Son of Man has authority on earth to forgive sins . . ." (Mark 2:11). The story is told not to give a journalistic account of an event but to teach Mark's audience what the event reveals about the iden-

INTERWEAVING OF MIRACLE STORIES AND
CONTROVERSIES IN MARK'S GOSPEL

I. Jesus' public ministry (Chapters 1–8)
   Jesus' identity is clear to the reader but not to Jesus' contemporaries

Mighty Signs
- 1:27 Exorcism
- 1:30 Cure of Simon's mother-in-law
- 1:33 Cure of many
- 1:40 Cure of leper
- 2:2 Cure of paralytic

Controversies
- 2:9 Controversy over power to forgive sin
- 2:17 Controversy over eating with sinners
- 2:18 Controversy over not fasting
- 2:23 Controversy over picking corn on the sabbath
- 3:2 Controversy over curing on the sabbath
- 3:5 Pharisees want to destroy Jesus
- 3:22 Controversy over exorcisms

Mighty Signs
- 4:40 Calming of storm
- 5:1 Curing of man with Legion
- 5:25 Cure of woman with hemorrhage
- 5:35 Cure of Jairus' daughter
- 6:37 First multiplication of the loaves
- 6:45 Jesus walks on water
- 6:55 Jesus heals the crowds

Controversy——7:1 Controversy over eating with unclean hands

Mighty Signs
- 7:24 Cure of Syrophoenician woman
- 7:37 Cure of deaf man
- 8:1 Second multiplication of the loaves

Controversy——8:10 Controversy over a "sign"

Mighty Sign——8:22 Cure of the blind man

II. Prelude to the passion (Chapters 9–13)
   At Peter's profession of faith Jesus starts to prepare his followers
   for his passion but they still do not understand.

Mighty Signs
- 9:2 Transfiguration
- 9:14 Cure of epileptic demoniac

Controversy——10:2 Controversy over divorce

Mighty Signs
- 10:46 Cure of blind Bartimaeus
- 11:12 Fig tree incident

Controversies
- 11:16 Pharisees want to kill Jesus
- 11:27 Controversy over authority
- 12:1 Controversy over rejecting Jesus
- 12:16 Controversy over paying taxes

III. Passion and resurrection
Controversy   14:1 Chief priests and scribes want to kill Jesus

tity of Jesus, an identity which was understood only after the resurrection.

Review Questions

1. Are all stories in the gospel the same literary form? Explain.
2. Did Jesus' mighty signs reveal his true identity to his contemporaries? Explain.
3. In Mark's gospel what is the function of a miracle story? How does the function of a miracle story affect its form?

Discussion Questions

1. Do you think Jesus worked mighty signs? Do you think there are mighty signs today? Do mighty signs "prove" anything? Explain.
2. Do you think it is "honest" of Mark to mold his stories to teach his audience a lesson rather than to function as an objective reporter? Explain.

ARTICLE 14

Tone Affects Meaning

Question: "Why was Jesus so rude to the Syrophoenician woman? What does he mean, 'Let the children first be fed, for it is not right to take the children's bread and throw it to the dogs' (Mark 7:24–30)? Is he calling the woman a dog? That's insulting." (Matthew 10:6 also discussed)

To answer these questions we need to look at both the content and the tone of Jesus' words.

First the content: The intent behind Jesus' comment is that it isn't fair to give to a non-Jew what was meant for the Jews. This in itself comes as a surprise to Gentiles who read Jesus' words centuries later. Modern day readers often forget to put Jesus' words into the historical context in which they were spoken.

The early church did not realize immediately that God intended to open up the covenant to the Gentiles. We read about how the early church came to this understanding in the Acts of the Apostles. But Jesus did not teach the disciples to go to the Gentiles. In fact, in Matthew's gospel Jesus is pictured as teaching the opposite.

"Do not turn your steps to pagan territory, and do not enter any Samaritan town; go rather to the lost sheep of the house of Israel" (Matthew 10:6).

Jesus seems to have understood his own ministry as one directed to the Jews. This woman was challenging him to expand his idea of his own ministry.

This interpretation suggests that Jesus faced the kind of challenge we all face. How many of us are slow to evangelize because

49

we think of the church as serving its own members? How many of us are slow to involve ourselves ecumenically because we think of the church as limited to our own denomination? Events force us to expand our vision. The same seems to have been true in Jesus' life.

Now the tone: To figure out the tone of something we read rather than hear, we must look at the passage in context. The way to judge Jesus' tone is to see what effect it had on the woman.

The woman certainly doesn't seem to be insulted. She must not have experienced Jesus' words as a put-down because she responds with real wit, "The house dogs under the table can eat the children's scraps." What can account for her response?

Some scripture scholars suggest that Jesus was using an idiom or a well-known phrase which was so familiar that it had no personal sting at all. This is always a possibility. Such an explanation often accounts for puzzling expressions in our culture. How would a scholar two thousand years from now explain someone saying, "I hope it rains cats and dogs," or reporting in the newspaper, "Mary Queen of Heaven Stomps Christ the King."? Socially accepted ways of speaking can certainly sound strange to another culture.

Even if Jesus were using an idiom so that his word choice was not offensive, wouldn't his intent have insulted the woman?

Obviously it didn't. It seems that Jesus was thinking out loud. He was letting the woman understand his problem—that he understood his mission to be for the Jews—and doing it with a kind of openness that invited her to persuade him otherwise, which she did.

Jesus' attitude could serve as a model both for Mark's audience and for us. In both cases our vision of who God wants us to be and what God wants us to do is constantly being challenged by events. Everyone is being invited to grow.

Review Questions

1. Why did Jesus have a problem with the woman's request?
2. How did Jesus respond, given the fact that he had a problem?

3. How do you determine the tone of something you read rather than hear?

Discussion Questions

1. Do you think Jesus was rude to the Syrophoenician woman? Why or why not?
2. Do you think the woman was insulted? Why or why not?
3. Are you surprised at the suggestion that Jesus grew in his idea of his own ministry? Why or why not?
4. Have events ever challenged you to reassess what you think God wants of you? Explain.

ARTICLE 15

Gospel Emphasis Meets Audience's Need

Question: "Why is it that Jesus, as he is pictured in Mark's gospel, seems to be 'on the edge' emotionally—not really in control of everything? He is angry a lot of the time (Mark 8:17–21), he curses that fig tree (Mark 11:14), and he actually prays not to have to go through with his suffering even though he knows he is going to rise from the dead (Mark 14:36). Why is this?"

The particular picture of Jesus which we get in Mark's gospel is formed by the needs of Mark's audience. Mark is editing the inherited oral and written traditions which have grown up in the community. He is selecting and molding this material so that it addresses the problems and questions which Mark's audience has.

Remember, Mark's audience was living under severe persecution. Those who originally read his gospel were literally having to choose between being faithful to their belief in the risen Christ or going into the Coliseum and being eaten by a lion.

It is not hard to imagine how one might rationalize the gospel message in such a way as to persuade oneself that Jesus did not want anyone to suffer and die.

For example, one might say, "Jesus healed. He would not want me to suffer." Or one might say, "Jesus taught that what is inside, in my heart, matters more than what I say. So it would be all right for me to say I don't believe in order to save my life because Jesus would know what is in my heart and that's what really matters."

Mark wants his audience to have the courage to choose death. How can he give them that courage? Mark holds Jesus up as an example. Jesus was in exactly the same situation as is Mark's

52

audience. In order to be faithful to his vocation Jesus had to face death.

Did Jesus find it easy? Of course not. At every turn Mark emphasizes just how hard Jesus found his life: how impatient he felt when the apostles failed to understand, how powerless he felt when people lacked faith, how angry he felt when he was tired and hungry, how full of dread he felt when the end was near. No one who reads Mark's gospel can think, "It was easy for Jesus because he was God." Rather, in reading Mark's gospel one forms just the opposite impression. Mark makes it clear that it was just as hard for Jesus to accept death as it would be for Mark's audience.

Shouldn't it have been easy for Jesus since he knew he would rise from the dead? Since the gospels include post-resurrection insights it is hard to know exactly what Jesus knew about himself while he was on earth. But knowledge of resurrection doesn't make death easy. If it did it would be easy for Mark's audience to die since they are post-resurrection people. The whole point of Mark's gospel is to assure his audience that suffering and death lead to life. The fact that suffering and death lead to life doesn't make them easy. It wasn't easy for Jesus either. Nevertheless, those who follow Jesus to death will find not death but life in the risen Lord.

Review Questions

1. Who is Mark's audience? What question do they have on their minds?
2. Why is it hard to know exactly what Jesus knew about himself while he was on earth?
3. What is the main theme of Mark's gospel?
4. Why does it suit Mark's purpose to emphasize the humanity of Jesus?

Discussion Questions

1. Is Jesus more or less appealing to you when you are confronted with his humanity? Explain.

2. What does the statement, "Jesus was like us in all things but sin," mean to you?
3. Does your belief in the resurrection free you from fear, impatience, dread or anger? Do you think your personal experience has any relevance to Jesus' experience? Why or why not?

ARTICLE 16

Who Is Inspired?

Comment: "Your articles on Mark's gospel are turning out to be a challenge to my faith. I don't like to think of the gospels as just inherited oral and written traditions which authors arranged for various audiences. You seem to me to be undercutting the idea that the gospels are inspired." (Luke 1:1–4 also discussed)

The person who made this comment reflected the thoughts and feelings which many experience when they first study the gospels. The statement reflects a very "healthy" faith because the person who made it is thoughtful, honest, and open. This person, who obviously feels a challenge to her previous understanding, does not want to run away from the challenge. She would rather work it through.

Let's start with the previous understanding. When we say, "The gospels are inspired," what do we think we mean?

Many people who believe in the inspiration of the Bible have a hard time answering this question. Do we believe that God actually wrote the gospels but Mark, Matthew, and Luke found them? No. Do we mean that God dictated the words in the gospel and then Mark, Matthew, and Luke wrote down the dictation? No. What role did the human "author" play?

I can't turn to Mark's gospel to respond to this question because Mark says nothing about his method. However, Luke does say something about his role as gospel author in the beginning of his gospel.

> Inasmuch as many have undertaken to compile a narrative
> of the things which have been accomplished among us, just
> as they were delivered to us by those who from the beginning

were eyewitnesses and ministers of the word, it seemed good
for me also, having followed all things closely for some time
past, to write an orderly account for you, most excellent
Theophilus, that you may know the truth concerning the
things of which you have been informed (Luke 1:1–4).

Notice that there is no claim of a spectacular experience here.
Luke says that he decided to write the gospel. Nor does Luke
claim that he witnessed the events about which he will write.
Rather Luke will base his account on what has been said and
written by those who preceded him.

Luke makes it clear that his gospel is the end product of a
process which started with events. Those who were eyewitnesses
of those events talked about them. However, they were not
journalists or historians. They were "ministers of the word."
They were people who served the believing community as
preachers, as teachers, and as presiders in liturgical settings.
Others before Luke—Mark and Matthew among them—had
drawn up written accounts based on the oral traditions. Luke has
gone over the sources available to him and has used some of
them as he wrote his own gospel.

So where does inspiration come in? Is Luke inspired? Is Mark?

The fact that Mark's gospel appears in the canon means that
the believing community has experienced Mark's work as inspired. However, that is not to say that Mark claims he was
inspired, that he knew he was inspired, that he had a vision, was
in a trance, or experienced life differently than we do.

A lot of you who are reading this book are inspired. Why are
you interested? What causes you to want to know more about
scripture? What is the source of that interest, maybe even that
longing, to be open to God's word? It is the Holy Spirit. We need
to expand the idea of inspiration which many of us have had in
regard to Mark, Matthew, and Luke to the church (i.e. the people of God) who preceded those three and to the church who has
come after them.

Those eyewitnesses of the events of Jesus' life who later recognized the significance of those events were inspired. The early
"ministers of the word" who faithfully served their communities

were inspired. Mark, Matthew, and Luke were inspired. The believing community which found itself spiritually fed through the gospels, and so cherished them and incorporated them into their life of prayer and worship, were inspired. And those who hunger and thirst for God's word today are inspired.

So the gospels aren't just inherited oral and written traditions edited to meet the needs of a contemporary audience. The word "just" doesn't fit. Nor are the gospel editors the only ones inspired. The gospels are the fruit of the Spirit who inspired the church at every stage of the process which resulted in the living word which we have today.

Review Questions

1. Does Mark claim a "supernatural" experience which resulted in his writing the gospel?
2. Is Mark the only inspired person who contributed to his gospel? Explain.
3. Why is Mark's gospel in the canon?

Discussion Questions

1. Is the idea that you might be inspired new to you? What do you think of this idea?
2. Has your idea of what "inspiration" means changed any since you started studying the gospels? Why or why not?
3. Do you think the Holy Spirit works through the whole community or just through a chosen few? Why? Does your knowledge of how the gospels came into existence affect your understanding of how the Holy Spirit works? Why or why not?

Summation and Transition
from Mark's to Matthew's Gospel

There are many questions which students have asked while reading Mark's gospel which we have not yet addressed. Many of these questions can be just as well posed in relation to another gospel.

It is now time to read Matthew's gospel. Some of the unanswered questions which have been asked in relation to Mark's gospel will be addressed in our discussion of Matthew's gospel.

In addition some of the methodology which we learned as we studied Mark's gospel can be applied to Matthew's: the importance of understanding literary form, of being attuned to irony, of putting Jesus' statements to individuals in the context of his relationship with those individuals. The more we learn to put what we read in the context in which it appears in each gospel, the more we will be able to understand the revelation which that gospel contains.

Obviously, to understand things in context we must read the whole gospel from beginning to end. Only then will we begin to see the gospel as a unified whole. As you read Matthew's gospel jot down every question which comes to your mind. Many of your questions will be addressed in the articles about Matthew's gospel which follow.

THE GOSPEL ACCORDING
to Matthew

ARTICLE 1

Gospel "Author" Is "Editor"

Question: "Why is so much of Mark's gospel repeated in Matthew?"

A great deal of Mark's gospel does reappear in Matthew. The reason is that Mark's gospel was one of the written sources which the editor of Matthew used as he collected his material.

Remember that the gospel "authors" are not so much authors as they are editors. Each gospel is an example of materials collected from a variety of oral and written traditions and arranged in a particular order to meet the needs of a particular audience.

Scripture scholars believe that the editor of Matthew had Mark's gospel in hand as he wrote his own gospel. However, the particular emphasis which Mark's gospel contains did not meet the needs of the audience which would be reading Matthew's gospel. The audience for Mark's gospel, you remember, were people suffering persecution who needed to understand why they should accept death rather than deny Christ. The audience for Matthew's gospel are not people facing persecution but people living in a settled Jewish community, probably Antioch, who want to understand how to integrate discipleship to Christ with their inherited Jewish traditions. Can one be both a faithful Jew and a faithful Christian? Or is embracing Christianity tantamount to turning one's back on Judaism?

In order to answer this question the editor of Matthew continually emphasizes his belief that Christ is the new Moses with authority from God to give the new law. As we look at a number of individual passages in Matthew's gospel we will see this em-

---

**FIVE THEMATIC SECTIONS
IN MATTHEW'S GOSPEL**

 I. Old law and new law
    A. Narrative 3:1–4:25
    B. Jesus' speech 5:1–7:29
 II. Instructions to disciples
    A. Narrative 8:1–9:34
    B. Jesus' speech 9:35–11:1
 III. The kingdom of God
    A. Narrative 11:2–12:50
    B. Jesus' speech 13:1–52
 IV. Community problems
    A. Narrative 13:53–17:27
    B. Jesus' speech 18:1–35
 V. Eschatology
    A. Narrative 19:1–23:39
    B. Jesus' speech 24:1–25:46

Preceded by the infancy narrative 1:1–2:23

Followed by the account of the passion, death and resurrection 26:1–28:20

---

phasis. However, the emphasis exists in the structure of the gospel as well as in the content.

Matthew's gospel is structured around five themes. Scripture scholars suggest that this structure is designed to reflect the five books of the Jewish law or torah. It appears that the editor of Matthew's gospel selected five topics with which he wished to deal: the relationship between the old law and the new law, Jesus' instructions to his disciples, the kingdom of God, community problems, and eschatology or the end times. Once these five topics were selected it appears that the editor of Matthew read through his sources and then "cut and pasted" the materials he found around his own five themes. That is why much of Mark's content appears in Matthew but not in the same order in which it appears in Mark.

In addition to Mark, scripture scholars believe that the editor of Matthew had other inherited sources. One source scholars refer to as "Q" is a collection of sayings which appears in both Matthew and Luke.

For each of his five themes the editor seems to have divided his material into two sections: a narrative section and a talk by Jesus. So in Matthew's gospel much of what Jesus has to say on a topic appears in one section. In Mark the same material might be sprinkled throughout the gospel.

The editor of Matthew prefaces his material on the five themes with an infancy narrative and follows it with an account of the passion, death, and resurrection.

Because the editor of Matthew has collated a variety of different kinds of writing we must remember that we have to consider the form of individual units in order to understand what we are reading. The stories originally existed as isolated units and had functions within the communities which composed them. As we grow in our ability to recognize these units and learn about their original functions we will grow in our ability to understand the revelation which is contained in Matthew's gospel.

Review Questions

1. Why is it more accurate to call the gospel "authors" gospel editors?
2. Who is Matthew's audience? What question is on their minds?
3. How is Matthew's gospel structured? Why?
4. Name two sources for Matthew's gospel.

Discussion Questions

1. Imagine that you are describing a party first to a best friend and next to a parent. Would the descriptions be identical? How does this relate to the gospels?
2. Imagine that you were going to give the good news of the gospel to two friends, one on death row and the other having

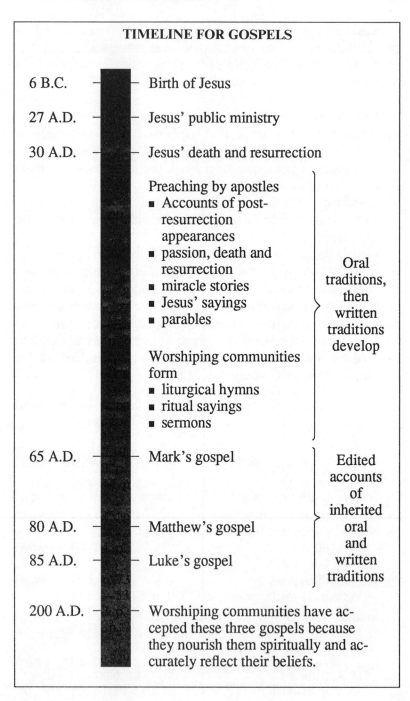

TIMELINE FOR GOSPELS

6 B.C. — Birth of Jesus

27 A.D. — Jesus' public ministry

30 A.D. — Jesus' death and resurrection

Preaching by apostles
- Accounts of post-resurrection appearances
- passion, death and resurrection
- miracle stories
- Jesus' sayings
- parables

Worshiping communities form
- liturgical hymns
- ritual sayings
- sermons

Oral traditions, then written traditions develop

65 A.D. — Mark's gospel

80 A.D. — Matthew's gospel

85 A.D. — Luke's gospel

Edited accounts of inherited oral and written traditions

200 A.D. — Worshiping communities have accepted these three gospels because they nourish them spiritually and accurately reflect their beliefs.

just celebrated the baptism of a child. Would you say the same thing to each person? How does this relate to the gospels?

THE GOSPEL ACCORDING TO MATTHEW

DATE	80 A.D.
AUDIENCE	Jewish Christians
SOURCES	Mark; "Q"; "M"
ORGANIZATION	An infancy narrative Five thematic sections each containing a narrative and a speech by Jesus An account of the passion, death and resurrection
THEME	Jesus is the new Moses with authority from God to give the new law
GOES BACK TO . . .	A genealogy to Abraham

ARTICLE 2

Infancy Narratives: Christological Stories

Question: "Why didn't Matthew tell us about the annunciation to Mary or that Jesus was born in a manger?"

The person who asked this question is already familiar with the Christmas story but is evidently noticing for the first time that the details of the story differ quite a bit between Matthew's and Luke's gospels.

In both Matthew and Luke we read the basic facts of the story: Mary and Joseph, who is of Davidic descent, were not yet married when Mary conceived a child through the Holy Spirit. The child's name was to be Jesus, and he would be a savior. Mary and Joseph were living together at the time of Jesus' birth in Bethlehem, during the reign of Herod the Great. Jesus was raised not in Bethlehem but in Nazareth.

However, only in Matthew do we read about the star, the magi, Herod's plot against Jesus, the massacre of the children, and the flight into Egypt. Luke says nothing about any of these points. Nor does Matthew mention details found in Luke: the annunciation to Mary, the birth in the manger or the announcement to the shepherds. Why do the two accounts differ in these details?

To answer this question we will have to ask ourselves, "What kind of writing are these infancy narratives? What is the intent behind them? How do these accounts relate to history?"

As you already know, the infancy narratives are not simply accounts of events written by family or friends at the time those events occurred.

Remember that when Jesus walked, talked and healed during

POINTS OF AGREEMENT IN MATTHEW'S AND LUKE'S INFANCY NARRATIVES

- Jesus' parents are Mary and Joseph.
- Mary and Joseph are engaged but not married at the time of Jesus' conception.
- Joseph is of Davidic descent.
- Mary conceives through the Holy Spirit.
- An angel directs that the child should be named Jesus.
- The angel says that Jesus is to be a savior.
- Jesus is born after Mary and Joseph are living together.
- Jesus is born in Bethlehem at the time of Herod the Great.
- Jesus is raised in Nazareth.

POINTS FOUND ONLY IN MATTHEW'S ACCOUNT

- The annunciation to Joseph
- The star
- The magi
- Herod's plot against Jesus
- The massacre of the children at Bethlehem
- The flight into Egypt

his public ministry his disciples simply didn't understand who he was. This was clear in Mark's gospel. There were no references to spectacular signs at Jesus' birth anywhere to be found.

After the resurrection Jesus' followers did begin to understand the significance of the events which had occurred. However, their interest in Jesus' life didn't revolve around his birth, but rather around the end of his life and his public ministry. Interest in Jesus' birth was a later development.

What are the ramifications of these facts? There are several. The first is that the intent behind the infancy narrative is not primarily historical but theological. The intent is not to give a detailed and realistic account of the events of Jesus' birth but to teach the theological significance of Jesus' birth in the lives of the readers.

Each gospel editor has retained the same core of historical events but has woven around this core a variety of details which are Old Testament images designed to teach a theological message.

In other words, each infancy narrative is a highly developed christological account which strives to answer not "What happened?" but rather "What are the ramifications of the events that have occurred in our midst?"

In order to understand how Matthew has answered that question for his audience we will have to figure out the theological significance of the details which he has included in his account,

Review Questions

1. How do the accounts of Jesus' birth differ in Matthew's and Luke's gospels?
2. Are the stories of Jesus' birth early or late developments in the gospel materials? Explain.
3. What question is each gospel editor trying to address in his infancy narrative?
4. What method does each gospel editor use in his infancy narrative?

Discussion Questions

1. Did you know that Matthew's and Luke's accounts differed? Does the fact that they differ distress you? Why or why not?
2. If you had been alive when Jesus was born and had witnessed a miracle, do you think that you would have drawn the conclusion that God had become man? Why or why not?
3. What is the difference between witnessing an event and understanding the ramifications of an event? Why is it often easier to understand the ramifications in hindsight?

ARTICLE 3

Infancy Narratives: Hindsight/Insight

Question: When did the three kings come? Jesus, Mary, and Joseph seem to have been living in a house at the time." (Matthew 2:11; Matthew 1:18–2:23 discussed)

The three kings are one of the details that appear only in Matthew's account of Jesus' birth. Since we now know that these details are Old Testament images woven around the account of events to teach Matthew's audience the theological significance of Jesus' birth we will have to reword this question in light of this knowledge.

The editor of Matthew's gospel doesn't want us to ask, "When did the three kings come?" If that is our question we have misunderstood the literary form of the infancy narratives. We have misunderstood the editor's intent. Rather he wants us to ask, "What is the theological significance of the image of the three kings? What is the significance of the star which they are pictured as following?"

To Matthew's audience the images of the star and the kings would have immediately recalled the beautiful song in Isaiah 60:

> Arise, shine: for your light has come,
>   and the glory of the Lord has risen upon you.
> For behold, darkness shall cover the earth,
>   and thick darkness the peoples;
> but the Lord will arise upon you,
>   and his glory will be seen upon you.
> And nations shall come to your light,
>   and kings to the brightness of your rising.

69

You shall suck the milk of nations,
  you shall suck the breast of kings;
and you shall know that I, the Lord, am your Savior
  and your Redeemer, the Mighty One of Jacob.
                              (Isaiah 60:1–3, 16)

As Matthew's audience read the images of the star and of the kings bringing gifts to Jesus, they would have understood that Matthew was identifying the baby born in Bethlehem, the historical Jesus, with Yahweh's saving presence.

Matthew was able to make this identification only in the light of the resurrection. But in hindsight the significance of Jesus' birth had become clear.

Matthew's account of Jesus' birth also includes the slaughter of the children and the flight into Egypt. Again Matthew, through images, is alluding to Old Testament events in order to enable his Jewish audience to understand the significance of Jesus' birth.

Herod's plot against Jesus and his attempt to kill Jesus by killing the children would have reminded Matthew's audience of the situation when Moses was born (see Exodus 1:15—2:10). Remember that Matthew, throughout his gospel, presents Jesus as the new Moses with authority from God to give the new law.

The story of Joseph, Mary and Jesus fleeing to Egypt would have reminded Matthew's audience of their patriarch Joseph (see Genesis 45:1–15). This story foreshadows the life of Jesus in so many ways: a child who is rejected by his own grows up to forgive and redeem his people.

By using Old Testament images to interweave the stories of Moses and Joseph with the story of Jesus' birth, Matthew allows his audience to see in the account of Jesus' birth what Jesus' contemporaries understood only after the resurrection. Jesus embodies the history of his people. In him all hope of redemption finds fulfillment. Jesus is the one who will forgive and save his people from their sins.

Thus we see that Matthew has used images to teach a deep,

post-resurrection, christological understanding of events to his Jewish audience.

Review Questions

1. Why is the question "When did the kings come?" an inappropriate question?
2. What is the editor teaching through the image of the three kings following the star?
3. What is the editor teaching through the image of the slaughter of the innocents?
4. What is the editor teaching through the image of the flight into Egypt?

Discussion Questions

1. If you wanted to teach that the baby Jesus' birth was light to the whole world, what images might you use?
2. Do you think that seeing the three kings in a manger scene will mean more or less to you now that you have read this article? Explain.

ARTICLE 4

"Fulfill": "Give Fuller Meaning"

Question: "What does Matthew mean when he says, 'All of this took place to fulfill the words of the prophet' (see Matthew 1:22; 2:6; 2:17; 3:3)? You'd think if everything was that clear-cut the Jews would have recognized Jesus as the Messiah." (Matthew 1:33 also discussed)

A modern day reader who is unfamiliar with the Old Testament might easily misunderstand both Matthew's intent and the function of a prophet when he or she reads, "All of this took place to fulfill the words of the prophet."

The errors which one might make upon reading these words are to conclude that a prophet was one who accurately predicted future events, and that the events of Jesus' life happened just as the prophet said they would.

When Matthew says, "All of this took place to fulfill the words of the prophet," he is not saying that the prophets foretold the events.

A prophet was not a fortune teller. In fact, fortune telling was prohibited by Jewish law. Rather, a prophet was a person of spiritual perception who was able to understand the ramifications of living in a covenant relationship.

A prophet looked at the situation of his contemporaries in the light of the fact that the Israelites were God's chosen people, and challenged his contemporaries to live up to their beliefs. If the people were sinning the prophet warned of trouble ahead. If the people were already in trouble the prophet offered hope in the light of God's faithful love.

Those who lived at the time of the prophet understood his

words in the context of their own lives and of their immediate future. The prophet's words were not understood as fortune-telling but as pointing out the ramifications of present behavior: "If you keep sinning you will bring disaster on yourself," or "Don't give up hope because God will once again send someone to save us."

So when Matthew uses the phrase "to fulfill the words of the prophet," he does not mean "fulfill" in the sense of a prediction fulfilled so much as in the sense of a hope fulfilled.

In addition to being fulfilled in the sense of a hope fulfilled, the words of the prophets are fulfilled in the sense that within them is discovered a deeper meaning than was intended by the prophet or understood by his contemporaries. This deeper meaning is seen only in the light of subsequent events and is thus attributed to the prophet's words only in hindsight.

For instance, Matthew quotes Isaiah when he says, " 'Behold, a virgin shall conceive and bear a son and his name will be called Emmanuel' (which means 'God with us')" (Isaiah 7:14; Matthew 1:33).

Modern readers with no knowledge of the Old Testament understand Matthew to be saying that Isaiah foretold both the virginal conception and the fact that God would become man.

Actually Isaiah foretold neither of these events. Historically, Isaiah the prophet said these words to King Ahaz who was putting his trust in political alliances rather than in Yahweh. Isaiah was reminding the king that he should trust God to save his people. He was offering hope by assuring King Ahaz that his line would continue: A young woman would conceive and bear Ahaz a son. God would be with this son as he had been with Israel's chosen leaders in the past.

By the time Matthew is writing, remarkable and unexpected events have occurred. A virgin has conceived through the power of the Holy Spirit and, in the light of the resurrection, that child is understood to have been God become man.

In the light of these events and post-resurrection insights Matthew sees a whole new level of meaning in the prophet's

PASSAGES IN WHICH MATTHEW REFERS TO FULFILLING THE WORDS OF THE PROPHETS	
1:22	12:17
2:15	13:14
2:17	13:35
2:23	21:4
4:14	26:54
5:17	26:56
8:17	27:9

words. "A virgin shall conceive" is now understood to refer to a conception without a human father, a conception in which the young maiden remains a virgin.

"God is with us" is now understood to mean that God became a human being. God is with us in a completely different way than Isaiah realized he would be. Thus the words of the prophet are fulfilled in the sense that they are given a fuller meaning.

Matthew's gospel is not pointing out to his Jewish audience that what they expected has now happened. Rather he is explaining that profoundly mysterious events have occurred in their midst, that God has gifted his people in a way that far exceeds their hopes or expectations, and that the words of the prophets can now be seen to have a whole new and much fuller meaning.

Review Questions

1. What was a prophet? What was his function?
2. If the prophets' words are not predictions, in what ways are the prophets' words fulfilled?
3. Explain two levels of meaning in the words, "A virgin shall conceive and bear a son and his name shall be Emmanuel."

Discussion Questions

1. Why do you think fortunetelling was against the Jewish law?
2. Can you think of anyone in American history or in contemporary times who has fulfilled the function of a prophet? Who? Why?

ARTICLE 5

Jesus, the New Moses,
Did Not Misuse Power

Question: "Was Jesus really tempted?" (Matthew 4:1–11; Matthew 27:41–42 also discussed)

Mark (1:12–13) Matthew (4:1–11) and Luke (4:1–13) all tell the story of Jesus' temptation. Since the questioner obviously has read an account of Jesus' temptation one wonders why the question has been asked.

Perhaps the questioner has such a clear idea of Jesus as God that it is hard to believe that Jesus experienced temptation. Perhaps the devil *tried* to tempt Jesus, but did Jesus actually experience temptation?

As we know, Mark emphasized the humanity of Jesus. Mark had good reason to let his persecuted audience see Jesus experience and overcome temptation.

Matthew keeps Mark's account and places the story in the material which precedes Jesus' sermon on the mount. Matthew precedes the sermon by a geneaology, a birth narrative, Jesus' baptism, and the temptation story. Each of these segments allows the reader to understand that Jesus really is the new Moses, the one to whom God has given authority to teach the new law.

In the story of the temptation Matthew shows that Jesus has overcome all temptations to misuse or abuse this God-given authority.

Jesus' first temptation (turn stones to loaves) is to use his power to satisfy his own needs, to serve his own desire. Even

76

though Jesus is very hungry he overcomes the temptation to self-gratification.

The second temptation (throw yourself from the pinnacle) is to use his power imprudently as a kind of showmanship—marvelous signs for their own sake with no message about the kingdom behind them. Jesus overcomes the temptation to make a meaningless spectacle of his power.

The third temptation (the possession of the kingdoms of the world) is to use his power to gain worldly or political dominance. Jesus overcomes this temptation and does not seek power on earth.

Self-gratification, the popularity of an entertainer, the power of political position—all are very tempting ways to use the kind of power which belonged to Jesus.

When you read the account of Jesus' passion and death in Matthew you will notice that Matthew and Mark both picture the chief priests mocking Jesus and saying, "He saved others; he cannot save himself. He is the king of Israel; let him come down now from the cross and we will believe in him" (Matthew 27:41–42; Mark 15:31–32).

The reader is not for an instant misled by such a "need for proof." The reader understands that Jesus long ago overcame the temptation to use his power in any way other than to fulfill the will of his Father. The reader knows Jesus will not save himself.

Again we have seen that we will miss a great deal of the meaning behind the gospel narratives if we approach the accounts with Jack Webb's "Just the facts" point of view.

Each gospel editor is arranging and molding his account to meet the needs of his audience. To understand the full intent of each account we must place it in the context of the author–audience relationship. Mark and Matthew each use this story, but each uses the story to emphasize something different. While Mark wants his persecuted audience to understand that Jesus too suffered temptation, Matthew wants his audience to see Jesus as the new Moses who never misused his God-given authority.

Review Questions

1. What temptations did Jesus overcome?
2. Why do the four segments in Matthew's gospel which precede the sermon on the mount prepare a Jewish audience to accept the sermon on the mount?
3. What is Mark's main point in telling the story of the temptation to his audience?
4. What is Matthew's main point in telling the story of the temptation to his audience?

Discussion Questions

1. Do you find it hard to think of Jesus actually experiencing temptation? Why or why not?
2. Other than the three ways mentioned, can you think of other temptations to abuse his power which Jesus might have experienced? What are they?

ARTICLE 6

The Challenge: Conversion of Heart

Question: "Why did Jesus tell people to mutilate themselves (Matthew 5:29–30; 18:8–9)? I think it would be wrong to cut off your hand or pluck out your eye." (Matthew 5:27–29; 8:21–22; 18:1–3 also discussed)

Jesus was a master teacher. As with the words of any master teacher, one has to put Jesus' words in context and invest them with tone in order to understand them. Jesus' words are aimed for specific audiences and emphasize certain points in order to respond to the needs of those audiences.

In Matthew's gospel the words, "If your right eye causes you to sin, pluck it out and throw it away," are preceded by the words, "You have heard that it was said, 'You shall not commit adultery.' But I say to you that every one who looks at a woman lustfully has already committed adultery with her in his heart" (Matthew 5:27–29).

The context in which a parallel passage appears (Matthew 18:8) is a conversation which begins with the disciples asking, "Who is the greatest in the kingdom of heaven?" Jesus responds, "Unless you turn and become like children, you will never enter the kingdom of heaven" (Matthew 18:1–3).

We see, then, that in each passage where the puzzling words in question appear Jesus is challenging his audience to a conversion of heart.

However, a conversion of heart is not the yardstick by which Jesus' audience is used to evaluating themselves from a religious point of view. Jesus' audience is used to asking not "Have I acted

79

lovingly?" but "Have I obeyed the law?" "Have I broken any of the rules?"

Jesus is constantly trying to teach people that holiness is not a matter of externals—washing your hands, merely avoiding evil actions. Rather, holiness is a matter of internals. What is in your heart?

Jesus' problem is: "How do I get these people to grow beyond their legalistic way of thinking? How do I get them to see that holiness is a matter of the heart?"

Jesus accomplishes his goal by triggering his audience's defense mechanisms. His words had exactly this same effect on the person who asked the question, "Wouldn't it be wrong to cut off my hand?"

Not only would it be wrong; it would be futile.

Jesus advises his listeners to cut off their hands *if* their hands cause them to sin.

But does a person's hand cause him or her to sin? Of course not. One could cut off both hands and both feet as well as pluck out both eyes and still sin. This is true because the cause of sin is not externals like hands, feet, and eyes, but internals. The cause of sin is lack of love in the heart.

Since Jesus' audience would respond to these words in self-defense they would, in a desire to preserve the wholeness of the body, argue themselves to the very position which Jesus is trying to teach. "If your hand causes you to sin . . ." "My hand does not cause me to sin. Sin comes from the heart."

As one learns to put Jesus' words in context and invest them with tone, other puzzling passages become clearer. For instance, why would Jesus tell that poor man whose father had died to leave the dead to bury the dead (Matthew 8:22)?

As with the passage about cutting off a hand, one has an immediate reaction of shock and resistance to this passage. It just doesn't seem right. Jesus is everywhere else compassionate to human suffering, especially to the suffering one experiences when one loses a loved one. What could Jesus mean?

Again we must put the words in context and invest them with tone.

Jesus says, "Leave the dead to bury their own dead," in response to a disciple who has said, "Lord, let me first go and bury my father" (Matthew 8:21–22). The man has not said that his father has died. He is suggesting that he not become a disciple as long as his father lives. He is using his father as an excuse for not following Jesus.

Jesus realizes that the man is making an excuse and uses the word "dead" to point this out. No one has died physically, but the disciple is in danger of dying spiritually.

These are just two examples of passages in which Jesus plays with words and says the unexpected in order to jar his listeners into reasoning their way to an insight which Jesus is trying to teach them.

Review Questions

1. What method should one use to try to figure out the meaning of a puzzling passage?
2. What is the "moral yardstick" Jesus' audience is accustomed to using?
3. What is the "moral yardstick" Jesus would like his audience to use?
4. How does Jesus' "advice" cause people to move to his point of view?
5. Why did Jesus say, "Leave the dead to bury the dead"?

Discussion Questions

1. Think about your own religious education. Were you taught to "examine your conscience"? What "yardstick" was used? What "yardstick" should be used?
2. What is your idea of sin? What do you think causes people to sin?
3. If a person sins and cutting off that person's hand won't help, what will help?

ARTICLE 7

Jesus; The Spirit; The Church

Question: "In Matthew's gospel, when Jesus teaches against divorce, he makes an exception (see Matthew 5:32; 19:9). What is the exception?" (Mark 10:11; Acts 15:29; 1 Corinthians 7:10–12; 15 also discussed)

It is true that in Mark we read, "Whoever divorces his wife and marries another commits adultery against her" (Mark 10:11), but the parallel passage in Matthew says, "Everyone who divorces his wife, except on the grounds of unchastity, makes her an adulteress" (Matthew 5:32).

What is the exception? Scripture scholars can't answer this question with certainty. English Bibles use a variety of words to translate the Greek word in question, including "fornication," "lewd conduct," "illicit marriage," "unfaithfulness," "unchastity," and "immorality." These words obviously have vastly different meanings. What is Matthew's exception?

In order to find an answer scholars ask, "What exception to the absolute teaching against divorce had become accepted in the early church by the time Matthew was writing (around 80 A.D.)? Perhaps it is such an exception which Matthew acknowledges.

New Testament writings provide two possible answers to this question. One is found in the Acts of the Apostles when we read about the decision made at the Council of Jerusalem (49 A.D.). The problem which confronted the early church at the time was, "Do Gentile converts have to become Jews in order to become Christians?" In other words, would a Gentile convert to Christianity have to observe all the Jewish laws?

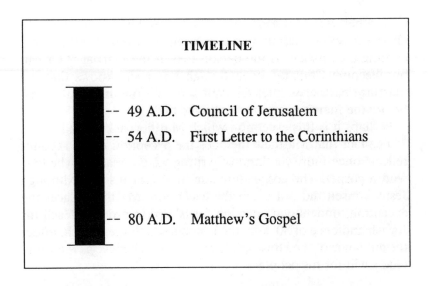

TIMELINE

-- 49 A.D.   Council of Jerusalem

-- 54 A.D.   First Letter to the Corinthians

-- 80 A.D.   Matthew's Gospel

In answer the apostles sent a letter to Antioch in which they said, "It has seemed good to the Holy Spirit and to us to lay upon you no greater burden than these necessary things: that you abstain from what has been sacrificed to idols, and from blood, and from what is strangled and from unchastity" (Acts 15:29).

The word translated "unchastity" here is thought to refer to marriages which violated the laws of consanguinity. For instance, could the marriage of a Gentile man to his blood sister be accepted as a marriage? The answer is "no." Perhaps Matthew was acknowledging this exception.

A second possibility appears in Paul's first letter to the Corinthians (54 A.D.). Paul too is trying to integrate the teaching against divorce with the problems at hand. Paul writes: "To the married I give charge, not I but the Lord, that the wife should not separate from her husband (but if she does, let her remain single or else be reconciled to her husband), and that the husband should not divorce his wife. To the rest I say, not the Lord, that if any brother has a wife who is an unbeliever, and she consents to live with him, he should not divorce her. . . . But if the unbelieving partner desires to separate, let it be so; in such a case the brother or sister is not bound. For God has called us to peace (1 Corinthians 7:10–12, 15).

In other words, if a person is forced by his or her spouse to choose between maintaining a marriage to an unbeliever or becoming a Christian, is the person tied in the marriage? Or can one become Christian even though he or she knows that the marriage partner will leave? Paul says that one may put Christ before the marriage and no longer be tied.

Perhaps it is this exception which Matthew acknowledges.

The fact that Matthew includes the exception in his account reflects once more the kind of writing we are reading when we read a gospel. The gospels include hindsight insight. Although Jesus himself did not teach the exception, Matthew places the exception, understood later, on Jesus' lips in order to teach his Jewish audience of 80 A.D. the insights which the church, under the guidance of the Holy Spirit, had come to believe as reflecting God's will for his people.

Review Questions

1. What is Matthew's "exception clause"?
2. What two possible answers does the New Testament offer to the question, "What exception to the absolute teaching against divorce had become accepted in the early church by the time Matthew was writing?"
3. What does the fact that Matthew feels free to place the exception on Jesus' lips tell you about the literary form of the gospel?

Discussion Questions

1. The apostles sent a letter to Antioch which said, "It has been decided by the Holy Spirit and by ourselves . . . ." What is the significance of beginning the letter in this way?
2. Do you think the early church had a right to decide the kinds of questions it was deciding? Why or why not?
3. Is the church still confronted with new problems? What are some? How should decisions be made?

ARTICLE 8

Prayer: Show or Worship?

Question: "Jesus says to pray in private (Matthew 6:6). Why should we worship with the community?" (Matthew 4:23; 5:14–16; 6:1–6; 9:35; 13:54; 18:20; 21:12; 21:14; 21:23; 26:55 also discussed)

To what degree should prayer and good works be private and to what degree should they be community activities? When we read Matthew's gospel we see warnings against the extremes of both options. The person who asked the question above is hearing only one side of the warning.

It is true that Matthew's gospel pictures Jesus as saying, "But when you pray, go into your room and shut the door and pray to your Father in secret" (Matthew 6:6). Is this a teaching against organized religion?

Of course not. It is a teaching against that kind of hypocrisy which uses the appearance of prayer to win worldly acclaim. Jesus makes his point perfectly clear by prefacing his statement with the words, "And when you pray, you must not be like the hypocrites; for they love to stand and pray in the synagogues and at the street corners, that they may be seen by men" (Matthew 6:5). It is against this hypocritical display that Jesus is teaching.

Jesus gives the same warning against acting for worldly acclaim in relation to good deeds. "Beware of practicing your piety before men in order to be seen by them; for then you will have no reward from your Father who is in heaven. . . . But when you give alms, your alms may be in secret" (Matthew 6:1, 4).

However, before we read these words on Jesus' lips we have already read: "You are the light of the world. A city set on a hill cannot be hid. Nor do men light a lamp and put it under a bushel, but on a stand, and it gives light to all in the house. Let your light so shine before men, that they may see your good works and give glory to your Father who is in heaven" (Matthew 5:14–16).

Are the two passages compatible? Yes, they are. We would all admit that there is all the difference in the world between a God-centered person who unself-consciously tries to serve God and others, and a self-centered person who self-consciously tries to serve self. Jesus is trying to teach his followers to live in the Father's love in all of their relationships so that others will also be drawn to the Father. Those who embrace religious practices to serve self rather than others can't bring others to the Father's love. The Father's love has nothing to do with their actions.

However, to say that *actions* might be visible to others is not to say that prayer would be. Should we pray only in secret?

Jesus himself recommends the power of praying with others when he says, "For where two or three are gathered in my name, there am I in the midst of them" (Matthew 18:20).

In addition, Jesus is pictured as setting the example of joining the community in their synagogues and temple. He taught in the synagogues in Galilee (Matthew 4:23), in the synagogues of all the towns and villages (Matthew 9:35), in the synagogues in Nazareth (Matthew 13:54), and in the temple in Jerusalem (Matthew 21:12, 14, 23; 26:55).

While Jesus wants to teach against and disassociate himself from the kind of hypocrisy and self-importance which can creep into peoples' religious practices, he still teaches us in both word and deed to participate not only in private prayer but in community prayer.

Review Questions

1. Against what fault is Jesus teaching when he advises people to pray in private?
2. What does Jesus mean when he says, "You are the light of the world"?

3. What evidence does Matthew's gospel offer that Jesus taught people to pray with others and prayed with others himself?

Discussion Questions

1. Do you see any value in praying with others? Explain.
2. Do you see any value in private prayer? Explain.
3. Think of the person on this earth whom you most admire. Describe that person. Do you know whether or not that person has a relationship with God? Explain.

ARTICLE 9

Prayer's Effect:
A Loving God Gives Good Things

Question: "Why did Jesus say, 'For everyone who asks receives' (Matthew 7:8)? We know from experience that this isn't true." (Matthew 6:7; 7:7; 7:11; 26:40; Luke 11:13 also discussed)

In the course of Matthew's gospel we read quite a few instructions on prayer. In addition we see Jesus himself pray while in deep distress. Are these various "lessons" on prayer compatible with each other? Are they compatible with our experience?

The questioner suggests that the words "Everyone who asks receives" are not compatible with our experience.

What is the passage teaching? When Jesus says, "Ask, and it will be given you; seek, and you will find; knock, and it will be opened to you" (Matthew 7:7), is he saying that *whatever* we ask for we will get even if it is not good for us or another? Of course not. This is evident from the context.

Two contexts are important for us to consider if we hope to understand the intent behind Jesus' words. The first is the fact that one's prayer is addressed to a loving Father; the second is that there is a "given" about that for which one is praying.

The reason Jesus teaches that the one who asks receives is that a loving Father hears and responds to the prayer. So in this passage Jesus is teaching about the attitude of trust we should have when we pray.

Because our prayers are directed to a loving Father we should pray with confidence that the response to our prayer will be that of a loving Father.

"If you then, who are evil, know how to give good gifts to your children, how much more will your Father who is in heaven give good things to those who ask him" (Matthew 7:11).

Jesus had earlier warned against "worried" prayers where one does not trust God's love. "And in praying do not heap up empty phrases as the Gentiles do; for they think that they will be heard for their many words. Do not be like them, for your Father knows what you need before you ask him" (Matthew 6:7). So when we pray we should do so with the confidence that a loving God hears and responds.

The second context in which we need to place the passage in question is that there is a "given" about that for which the person is asking. Jesus said, "How much more will your Father who is in heaven give *good things* to those who ask him" (Matthew 7:11). The parallel passage in Luke is even more precise, for in it Jesus says, "How much more will the heavenly Father give the *Holy Spirit* to those who ask him" (Luke 11:13)?

So Jesus isn't saying that the person who asks will always get that for which the person has asked. Rather he is saying that the person who asks should be confident that his or her prayer will be heard by a loving Father who will respond for that person's good.

Jesus not only taught others how to pray but he prayed himself. So part of what Matthew has to say about prayer can be seen from looking at Jesus' prayer. During the most painful time of Jesus' life Matthew pictures Jesus as saying, "My Father, if it be possible, let this cup pass from me; nevertheless, not as I will, but as thou wilt" (Matthew 26:40). In this prayer we see Jesus doing exactly what he taught others to do when he said, "Ask and you will receive."

Jesus' prayer is definitely a prayer of petition. He is asking to be relieved of the pain which will be inflicted on him by those who object to the truths which he has so faithfully taught.

However, even as Jesus asks for something very specific he does so in full confidence that his Father loves him and that the response from his Father will be for the best. He also assumes that the loving Father is a better judge of what is for the best than he is. That is why Jesus can honestly pray, "Let it be as you, not I would have it" (Matthew 26:40).

Jesus' teaching on prayer, once understood, is not incompatible with our experience or his. Jesus is not teaching that by asking we can get anything we want. Rather he is teaching that when we pray in love and trust to a loving Father, God's response will be for our good.

Review Questions

1. What is Jesus teaching when he says, "Ask, and it will be given to you"?
2. Does Jesus practice what he preaches when it comes to prayer?
3. What belief lies behind a person's ability to pray, "Not my will but yours be done"?

Discussion Questions

1. Do you think prayer makes any difference? Why or why not?
2. Have you ever had a prayer experience that made you confident of God's love, power and presence? Explain.

ARTICLE 10

Parables: To Hide or To Reveal the Truth?

Question: "Why did Jesus teach in parables? Was he trying to hide or reveal the truth?" (Matthew 13:10–15, 34–35; 21:28)

There are two places in the thirteenth chapter of Matthew's gospel that address the question, "Why does Jesus teach in parables?"

The first passage is extremely puzzling. After Jesus tells the parable of the sower the disciples ask him, "Why do you speak to them in parables?" Jesus replies, "To you it has been given to know the secrets of the kingdom of heaven, but to them it has not been given. . . . This is why I speak to them in parables, because seeing they do not see, and hearing they do not hear, nor do they understand. With them indeed is fulfilled the prophecy of Isaiah which says:

'You shall indeed hear but never understand,
  and you shall indeed see but never perceive.
For this people's heart has grown dull,
  and their ears are heavy of hearing.
  and their eyes they have closed,
lest they should perceive with their eyes,
  and hear with their ears,
and understand with their heart,
  and turn for me to heal them' " (Matthew 13:10–15).

At first glance this is a very puzzling passage. Could it be that Jesus teaches in parables to hide the truth, for otherwise people might hear and understand, be converted and forgiven?

To interpret the passage in this way puts it in direct contradiction to a passage which appears just a little later in the same chapter. "All this Jesus said to the crowds in parables; indeed he said nothing to them without a parable. This was to fulfill what was spoken by the prophet;

'I will open my mouth in parables,
    I will utter what has been hidden since the foundation of the
        world' " (Matthew 13:34–35).

In this passage it seems that Jesus teaches in parables to reveal, not to hide the truth. Through parables Jesus reveals truths never before heard or understood.

Are the passages contradictory? Did Jesus teach in parables to reveal or to hide the truth?

In order to attack this problem let's move away from these verbal responses to the question "Why does Jesus teach in parables?" and look instead at what Jesus does.

We see many instances of Jesus teaching in parables in Matthew's gospel. Many of these parables begin, "The kingdom of God is like . . . ." Through the parables Jesus is trying to teach about something mysterious—"the kingdom of God"—by comparing it to something well known: a mustard seed, yeast, a man who discovers treasure in a field, etc.

So in these instances Jesus is teaching in parables in order to reveal a truth, one which is outside the material world and therefore not easily accessible to us since we learn through our five senses.

Still other parables are directed to a very specific audience. The parable of the two sons (Matthew 21:28) begins with the words "What is your opinion? A man had two sons . . ." and is addressed to the chief priests and elders of the people who have questioned Jesus' authority. This is an example of a parable told to a resistant and defensive audience that is antagonistic to Jesus' message and his person.

Examples of parables addressed to resistant audiences might

help us understand why Jesus would say that he teaches in parables because his audience "looks without seeing and listens without hearing." Parables are a brilliant way to get around the defenses of a resistant audience.

When resistant people first hear the parable they do not realize that Jesus is telling a story which will end up by criticizing them. Since they see no connection between themselves and the characters in the story they get involved in the story and pass judgment on the characters. Only in hindsight do they realize that they have passed judgment on themselves.

So Jesus tells parables to reveal the truth. Sometimes that truth is about the spiritual world which is beyond the audience's knowledge and perception. Sometimes that truth is about the audience itself that is too resistant to hear the truth unless it is presented in the form of a parable.

Review Questions

1. What does Jesus mean when he says he teaches in parables because his audience listens but does not hear?
2. What does the collator of Matthew's gospel mean when he says that Jesus teaches in parables to reveal hidden truths?
3. Why does Jesus teach in parables?

Discussion Questions

1. Why is it difficult to teach anything about the spiritual world?
2. Can you think of any way that a person can point out a fault of yours without your taking offense? What does this question have to do with parables?

ARTICLE 11

"Christ": What Does the Word Mean?

Question: "Did Peter understand who Jesus was or not? Peter says, 'You are the Christ, the Son of the living God.' But then he starts to argue with Jesus and Jesus calls him 'Satan.' What's going on here?" (Matthew 16:13–23; Matthew 8:27–33; 16:5–9; 16:18; Mark 8:27–33 also discussed)

It is clear in both Mark's and Matthew's gospels that the apostles did not really understand who Jesus was until after the resurrection. Their ignorance is softened slightly in Matthew's account but not hidden.

The disciples' inability to understand is never more evident than it is in the passage immediately preceding Peter's words, "You are the Christ" (see Matthew 16:5–9). In this passage Jesus warns the disciples about the negative influence of the Pharisees by saying, "Take heed and beware of the leaven of the Pharisees and Sadducees." The disciples, who had forgotten to bring any bread with them, are worried about their stomachs. They misunderstand Jesus' metaphor, "yeast," and say, "We brought no bread." Jesus is exasperated, to say the least.

In the very next scene we see Jesus ask the disciples, "Who do men say that the Son of Man is?" (Matthew 16:13). Simon Peter then says, "You are the Christ" (Matthew 16:16). The word "Christ" is a synonym for the word "messiah." Both words mean "the anointed one." Peter is professing his faith and his understanding that Jesus is the messiah.

However, what Peter meant by the word "Christ" and what we mean by the word "Christ" are not the same. To understand

94

this scene we must resist the mistake of projecting our knowledge and our meaning of the word "Christ" onto Peter's words.

When Peter said, "You are the Christ," he meant that he thought Jesus was the anointed one of God whom the Jews were expecting to defeat their political enemies and free them from political bondage. He meant that Jesus was the Son of God as Moses and David were sons of God—chosen instruments of God's power and presence among his people. Peter did not understand his words in the same way that we understand them.

This is evident from what follows. Jesus understands Peter's expectations of the messiah. He wants to let Peter know that he is right—Jesus is the expected one—but that what the Jews were expecting and what they were getting in Jesus were not the same. Instead of getting a political king messiah they were getting a suffering messiah.

So Jesus accepts the idea that he is the messiah by calling himself "Son of Man," a messianic title. However, Jesus tells his disciples that the Son of Man was destined to suffer and die. At this point Peter's comprehension breaks down completely. He simply cannot understand or accept the idea that if Jesus was indeed the messiah, instead of reigning he would die. It is at this point that Peter argues with Jesus. "God forbid, Lord. This shall never happen to you" (Matthew 16:22).

Jesus gets very angry with Peter. Jesus calls Peter "Satan," and says, "You are a hindrance to me; for you are not on the side of God but of men" (Matthew 16:23).

Why is Jesus so angry? He seems to have experienced Peter's words as a temptation. Jesus did not want to die. The last thing he needed was for Peter to tempt him to avoid his destiny. So Jesus calls Peter a "Satan."

It is interesting to note that while Matthew is willing to repeat this episode found in his source, Mark (see Mark 8:27–33), he does so in such a way as not to undercut Peter's authority in the minds of his audience.

Remember that Matthew is writing to settled Jews and is everywhere interested in establishing Jesus' authority as the new Moses. By the time Matthew is writing (80 A.D.) Jesus' authority is exercised in the authority of the early church leaders. So before he repeats this distressing scene between Jesus and Peter, Matthew inserts the passage in which Peter's authority is confirmed. "You are Peter and on this rock I will build my church" (Matthew 16:18). But the faith, knowledge and spiritual insight which Peter eventually develops in order to fulfill his role are not with him at this point in his life.

Peter's lack of real understanding makes Jesus' admonition to silence understandable. "Then he strictly charged the disciples to tell no one that he was the Christ" (Matthew 16:20).

Why silence? Because the apostles couldn't explain to others what they didn't understand themselves. Jesus realized that while they could use the word "Christ," they did not yet understand what that word actually meant when applied to him.

Review Questions

1. What is Jesus teaching when he says, "Be on your guard against the yeast of the Pharisees"?
2. What did Peter mean when he said, "You are the Christ"?
3. How did Jesus try to correct Peter's understanding of what the messiah would be?
4. Why did Jesus get angry with Peter?
5. Why did Jesus tell the apostles not to tell anyone about him?

Discussion Questions

1. In your experience have your expectations been fairly accurate to the reality which followed? Explain. How does this relate to the gospels?
2. Can you think of anything you understood gradually so that if you passed on your early understanding you would be wrong? Explain. How does this relate to the gospel?

ARTICLE 12

"Kingdom": What Is It?

Question: "Why did Jesus tell his disciples that some of them would not taste death 'before they see the Son of Man coming in his kingdom' (Matthew 16:28)? In hindsight we know he was wrong." (Matthew 16:27; 1 Corinthians 7:29ff; 2 Thessalonians 3:10–11 also discussed)

First I'd like to reword this question. Instead of saying "Why did Jesus tell his disciples . . . ?" it would be more accurate to say "Why did the editor of Matthew's gospel picture Jesus as telling his disciples . . . ?"

By rewording the question in this way we acknowledge the fact that we cannot assume that all words attributed to Jesus are exact quotations. Since the written gospel consists of the inherited oral and written traditions of the early church, it includes the church's hindsight insight. Ideas understood later are sometimes placed on Jesus' lips in order to make them clear to the contemporary audience.

This distinction does not in any way lessen the pertinence of the question. The presumption behind the question is that Jesus taught his disciples that the "end of the world" would come in their lifetime. This impression is even stronger when the verse in question is read in its context.

Jesus has just finished telling his disciples that he will suffer death and then be raised. After several other admonitions about "taking up their crosses" and following him, Jesus says: "For the Son of Man is to come with his angels in the glory of his Father, and then he will repay every man for what he has done. Truly, I say to you, there are some standing here who will not taste death

before they see the Son of Man coming in his kingdom"
(Matthew 16:27–28).

It seems that Jesus' contemporaries did expect the "end of the
world," the "second coming," imminently. This is reflected in
Paul's letters when he advises those who are unmarried to remain that way because "our time is growing short. . . . The world
as we know it is passing away" (1 Corinthians 7:29ff). The same
misunderstanding is apparent when Paul admonishes those who
are not working to get to work (2 Thessalonians 3:10–11). Evidently the Thessalonians were not sure that the second coming
had not already occurred. If the second coming were going to
happen any minute, why go looking for a wife or a job?

In hindsight we know that the world, as Paul knew it, did not
pass away after all. What are we to make of this? Did Jesus
misunderstand? Did those who heard Jesus misunderstand what
he said? Are we misunderstanding what Jesus said?

Biblical critics through the years have suggested that Jesus was
not referring to the end of the world in this passage but to the
destruction of Jerusalem which occurred in 70 A.D. This would
have preceded Matthew's Gospel by some ten years.

Another way to approach the problem is to ask, "What does
Jesus mean by the word "kingdom"? Are "the end of the world"
and "the coming of the kingdom" synonyms?

In all that Jesus says about the coming of his kingdom and
about the second coming Jesus speaks in images. Perhaps the
problem lies with the fact that his original audience and succes-
sive generations have taken his images too literally.

The questioner is presuming that the kingdom has not yet
come. Is this true?

The answer depends entirely on how one understands the
word "kingdom." The disciples understood the word to refer to a
geopolitical entity. They expected Jesus to be a king like David.

Jesus seems to be using the word "kingdom" as a metaphor to
describe a spiritual reality, a reality which already exists and
which he is making accessible to his people.

Is the kingdom something which exists outside a person or

within a person? Is it a present or future reality? Does one enter it through physical death or through conversion of heart?

Much of Matthew's gospel is devoted to teachings about the kingdom of heaven. Jesus tried to help his listeners understand what he meant by kingdom by telling parables which draw numerous comparisons. As we study some of these parables we will be more able to answer the question, "Has the kingdom come or not?"

Review Questions

1. Does the Gospel claim exact quotations? Explain.
2. Did the early Christians expect the end of the world soon? How do you know?
3. What did the disciples mean by the word "kingdom"?
4. What did Jesus mean by the word "kingdom"?
5. How does Jesus teach about the kingdom?

Discussion Questions

1. What does the word "kingdom," as Jesus used it, mean to you?
2. Do you think the kingdom is a present or a future reality? Why?

ARTICLE 13

Forgiveness: A Must

Question: "What is Jesus really teaching about forgiveness? First he says that if your brother does something wrong and persists in not listening after this has been pointed out to him, then he should be treated "as a Gentile and a tax collector" (Matthew 18:15–17). But then he tells Peter he must forgive "seventy times seven" (Matthew 18:22). Aren't these contradictory teachings? (Matthew 6:12–15; 18:23–35 also discussed)

To forgive others from the heart seems to be essential to Christ's teaching. After all, God has forgiven us so we must forgive others. Jesus makes this clear on many occasions. The parable of the unforgiving debtor (Matthew 18:23–35) is a case in point.

Notice how the parable begins: "Therefore, the kingdom of heaven may be compared to a king who wished to settle accounts with his servants" (Matthew 18:23). This is one of those many parables which teaches something about the kingdom.

The parable then continues to describe a situation in which a servant who had already been forgiven by his king, refuses to forgive a fellow servant. On hearing this the king sends the servant to jail.

What does this parable teach about the kingdom? Apparently, to forgive others is necessary if one wants to be in the kingdom.

Jesus' words to Peter about forgiving seventy times seven reaffirm this truth.

This same teaching on the relationship between our willingness to forgive others and our receiving God's forgiveness had previously been taught in the Our Father: ". . . And forgive us

our debts, as we have forgiven those who are in debt to us."
(Matthew 6:12) and had been emphasized at the end of that
prayer. "For if you forgive men their trespasses, your heavenly
Father also will forgive you; but if you do not forgive men their
trespasses, neither will your Father forgive your trespasses
(Matthew 6:14–15).

What, then, are we to make of the teaching that one who
persists in wrongdoing, even when corrected by the community,
should be treated "like a Gentile or a tax collector?"

The question, "How often should I forgive?", and the question, "What should I do if my brother does something wrong?",
are different questions.

To correct a brother who is doing something wrong is to act
for his good. Jesus makes this clear when he says, "If he listens to
you, you have won back your brother" (Matthew 18:15). If he
does not listen and so you correct him in the company of one or
two others, and finally in the presence of the community you are
still acting for his good. The goal is still to win your brother back.

If the person still fails to listen what should be done? To treat
him, "as a Gentile or a tax collector," as one who is not a
member of the community, is not to fail to forgive. After all,
Jesus constantly offered forgiveness to pagans and tax collectors.
Rather it is to acknowledge by one's behavior that such wrongdoing separates one from the community. However, the goal in
acting this way is still to win the person back. Perhaps this
treatment will enable him to see the error of his ways, and to
repent.

If the person should repent, the community is bound to forgive and welcome that person back. The option of refusing forgiveness does not exist if one wishes to be Jesus' disciple and to
live in the kingdom.

Review Questions

1. What is Jesus teaching about the kingdom in the Parable of
   the Unforgiving Debtor?
2. What is Jesus teaching Peter when he says, "You must forgive
   seventy times seven?

3. What is taught about correcting others?
4. Are the teachings about forgiveness and the teaching about correction compatible? Explain.

Discussion Questions

1. Do you really believe that everyone is a forgiven sinner? Why or why not?
2. Does the thought that you are a forgiven sinner persuade you that you should forgive others? Why or why not?
3. Do you regard it as a good or bad thing to do to correct someone who is choosing to do wrong? Explain.
4. How did Jesus treat "Gentiles and tax collectors"?

ARTICLE 14

Jesus Uses Hyperbole

Question: "Why did Jesus say that it is easier for a camel to pass through the eye of a needle than for a rich man to enter heaven (Matthew 19:24)? Does one have to be poor to be Christian?" (Matthew 5:5; 6:19–21, 24; 7:3; 19:16; 19:20–21; 23:24 also discussed)

As always, the passage in question must be read in context for one to hope to understand its meaning.

Jesus has just had a conversation with a rich young man. The man has asked, "Teacher, what good deed must I do, to have eternal life?" (Matthew 19:16). Jesus tells the young man to keep the commandments. However, the young man persists and says, "All these I have observed; what do I still lack?" (Matthew 19:20).

Jesus then says, "If you would be perfect, go, sell what you possess and give to the poor, and you will have treasure in heaven, and come follow me" (Matthew 19:21).

At this point the young man does not accept the invitation to discipleship. Rather, he goes away. In other words, this young man was so attached to his wealth that it stood between him and discipleship.

Having just witnessed this scene, Jesus points out to his disciples the obvious—it is harder to say "yes" to discipleship if that "yes" involves giving up material wealth.

But is it impossible to be rich and a disciple? After all, it is impossible for a camel to pass through the eye of a needle.

Some commentators suggest that "the eye of a needle" was the name of a gate to the Jerusalem market. For a camel, laden with

103

goods, to pass through this gate would have been difficult but not impossible.

Other commentators point out that no evidence for the existence of such a gate at the time Jesus lived has been found. Such a gate after Jesus' time could just as well have been named after the saying.

Jesus' choice of words here might be better understood if compared to something he says later to the Pharisees when he is angry at them for scrupulously paying attention to minute details of the law while completely ignoring the whole point of the law. He says, "You blind guides, straining out a gnat and swallowing a camel" (Matthew 23:24).

Jesus uses the same kind of hyperbole or exaggeration when he teaches the crowds not to judge others. "Why do you see the speck that is in your brother's eye but do not notice the log that is in your own eye?" (Matthew 7:3).

Perhaps Jesus is using this same kind of hyperbole to make a point when he uses the phrase "easier for a camel to go through the eye of a needle."

To suggest that Jesus is using hyperbole is not to suggest that he does not sincerely mean what he is teaching. Jesus had earlier warned against accumulating possessions on earth when he said, "Do not lay up for yourselves treasures on earth, where moth and rust consume and where thieves break in and steal, but lay up for yourselves treasures in heaven, where neither moth nor rust consumes and where thieves do not break in and steal. For where your treasure is, there will your heart be also. . . . No one can serve two masters; for either he will hate the one and love the other, or he will be devoted to the one and despise the other. You cannot serve God and mammon" (Matthew 6:19–21, 24).

The apostles are amazed at this teaching. They had previously viewed material success as a blessing from God, a sign of God's favor. To look on material possessions as a possible detriment to one's spiritual life came as a total surprise to them.

Is it then impossible to put God first if one is rich? No, it isn't. But to do so is very difficult. However, with God all things are possible, even the difficult task of keeping material possessions in their proper order in the hierarchy of things.

Such a graced person might be a good steward of riches, a true disciple of Christ, using his or her resources to help those in need. Such a person might well identify with Jesus' words, "Blessed are the poor in spirit, for theirs is the kingdom of heaven" (Matthew 5:3).

Review Questions

1. In what context did Jesus say, "It is easier for a camel to pass through the eye of a needle than for a rich man to enter heaven"?
2. What is hyperbole? Give several examples of Jesus' use of hyperbole.
3. Why are the apostles so surprised by Jesus' remarks on the danger of riches?
4. What is the danger of riches?

Discussion Questions

1. Do you think the average American reflects gospel values in the way he or she uses material resources? Why or why not?
2. What do you think Jesus meant when he said, "How happy are the poor in spirit; theirs is the kingdom of heaven"?
3. Do you think one has to be poor to be Christian? Why or why not?

ARTICLE 15

The Kingdom: A Gift

Question: "I agree with the vineyard workers who complained that they weren't paid more than those who worked a shorter time. What is Jesus teaching in this parable?" (Matthew 20:1–16)

Many people react to the parable of the vineyard workers just as this questioner did. When we listen to this story, in which laborers who worked all day were paid no more than those who came near the end of the day, many feel sympathetic for those who worked longer. "Those who worked longer should have been paid more," is an opinion that sums up not only the reaction of the all day workers themselves but of many readers as well.

What is Jesus teaching in this parable? Usually when we identify with those who get corrected in a parable it is because we share the fault or the misunderstanding which Jesus is criticizing in his audience through the story.

In order to explain this further let's first back up and talk about a method for parable interpretation. A parable is a specific kind of writing, a specific literary form, different from other literary forms such as legends, allegories, miracle stories, etc. Each form has its own function and demands its own method of interpretation.

A parable has the function of challenging, of correcting, of calling to conversion the person or people to whom the story is told. So in order to interpret a parable we must ask ourselves to whom the story is addressed and what precipitated the story.

In other words, a parable is the middle of a conversation. In

---

METHOD FOR PARABLE INTERPRETATION

A Parable: Look for one basic comparison between an element in the story and the audience listening to the story. The lesson comes from this comparison. Ask yourself:
- To whom is Jesus speaking?
- What's the topic?
- With what person or thing in the story does the audience compare?
- What lesson is drawn from this comparison?

---

order to understand the middle of a conversation one must go back and put that part of the conversation in context.

Once we determine the person or people to whom the parable is addressed we should ask ourselves, "To whom in the story does this audience compare?" There will be some character in the story (or less often some thing) who is similar to the audience in some way. It is through this comparison that the parable criticizes and challenges the audience.

This will all become clear with an example. To whom is Jesus speaking when he tells the parable of the vineyard workers?

If we look before the parable we find the conversation which precedes the story. Peter has said to Jesus, "Lo we have left everything and followed you. What then shall we have?" (Matthew 19:27).

In response to this question Jesus tells the parable which begins, "The kingdom of heaven is like . . . ."

So through the parable Jesus is responding to Peter's question. What is he teaching Peter about the kingdom of God?

Behind Peter's question there is a false presumption. To paraphrase, Peter is as much as asking: "What have we earned?"

Peter and the disciples compare to the vineyard workers. They have certain expectations about what they should earn. But those expectations are challenged, not because the owner of the

---

**A COLLECTION OF PARABLES ABOUT THE
KINGDOM IN MATTHEW'S GOSPEL**

Each gives us just a glimpse of the truth behind the image

Mt 13:24–30	Parable of the Darnel
Mt 13:31–32	Parable of the Mustard Seed
Mt 13:33	Parable of the Yeast
Mt 13:44	Parable of the Treasure
Mt 13:45	Parable of the Merchant
Mt 13:47–50	Parable of the Dragnet
Mt 18:23–35	Parable of the Unforgiving Debtor
Mt 20:1–16	Parable of the Vineyard Laborers
Mt 21:33–43	Parable of the Wicked Husbandmen
Mt 22:2–14	Parable of the Wedding Feast
Mt 25:1–13	Parable of the Ten Bridesmaids
Mt 25:14–30	Parable of the Talents

---

vineyard paid some less than they earned, but because he was too generous. The injustice, if there was one, was that some people got more than they earned.

What, then, does the story teach Peter about the kingdom of heaven? Through this story Jesus is surfacing and challenging Peter's presupposition that his "reward" will be what he has "earned." The kingdom of heaven is not "earned." No one "earned" the right to work in the vineyard in the first place. Rather each person was there by invitation. The kingdom is a gift.

If one were to think in terms of "earning" one would not receive less than he deserved. But the whole concept of "earning" is inappropriate when thinking about the kingdom.

In addition to showing Jesus teaching Peter that the kingdom is a gift, the editor of Matthew's gospel may well have been addressing a problem on the minds of his Jewish audience.

By the time Matthew's gospel is being collated, Gentiles have been accepted into the covenant community. As was mentioned in an earlier article, the original audience may well have been expecting "the end of the world" soon. They may well have been wondering how it is that the Jewish people, who have been involved in a covenant relationship with Yahweh for two thousand years, should now find Gentiles welcomed into the covenant relationship on an equal footing with them. Matthew may well be reminding his Jewish audience that the kingdom is a gift to Jew and Gentile alike. Neither "earned" the kingdom. Each was chosen. Those who were invited into the vineyard near the end of the day (the Gentiles) are treated just as generously by the land owner as those who were invited first (the Jews).

By including this parable in his gospel, Matthew has succeeded in challenging the assumptions of succeeding generations. Like Peter, many of us need to be reminded that we are not earning the kingdom. Rather we are being gifted by an overly generous God.

Review Questions

1. What three questions should we ask ourselves in order to interpret a parable correctly?
2. In response to what question of Peter's did Jesus tell the parable of the vineyard workers?
3. To what character in the parable does Peter compare?
4. What about the kingdom of God is Jesus teaching Peter through this parable?
5. What is Matthew teaching his contemporaries through this parable?

Discussion Questions

1. How do you react to the parable of the vineyard laborers? Do you sympathize with anyone? Whom? Why?
2. Do you think you "earn" grace? Heaven? Why or why not?
3. Can you think of anything you have "earned" that isn't the result of your having been gifted by God? Explain.

ARTICLE 16

The Kingdom: Response Required

Question: "Why did that poor guy get thrown out of the wedding feast? After all, it wasn't his fault that he wasn't dressed properly." (Matthew 22:1-14; Matthew 7:21; 21:28-39 also discussed)

In order to respond to this question let us follow the method of parable interpretation which we have already discussed. The parable is the middle of a conversation. So we need to ask ourselves, "To whom is Jesus telling this story? What precipitated the story? What character in the story is like the audience in some way? What fault in the audience is being criticized through this comparison?"

Only after answering these questions can we hope to understand what Jesus is teaching his audience and us through the parable.

The parable of the wedding feast is the third parable in a row told to the Pharisees after they question Jesus' authority. The Pharisees can't stand Jesus. Jesus knows how they feel about him and that they are completely closed to his teaching. Because the Pharisees are such a resistant audience Jesus uses parables in an attempt to work around their defenses.

In the first parable Jesus tells a story of two sons, one who says he will not do his father's will but does, the second who says he will do his father's will but does not (Matthew 21:28-31). Jesus is comparing the Pharisees to this second brother. They appear to say "yes" to the Father, but in reality they fail to do the Father's will.

In the second parable Jesus tells a story of the wicked tenants who abuse the servants of the vineyard owner and then kill his sons (Matthew 21:33–39). Jesus invites the Pharisees to pass judgment on these wicked tenants when he says, "When therefore the owner of the vineyard comes, what will he do to these tenants?" (Matthew 21:40). The Pharisees reply that the vineyard will be taken away from them and given to others.

After the Pharisees pass judgment on the wicked tenants, they realize that they have been tricked into passing judgment on themselves. The kingdom will be taken away from them. They then want to arrest Jesus.

The conversation continues with the parable of the marriage feast (Matthew 22:1–14). In this parable Jesus is warning the Pharisees that not all who are invited to the wedding feast and who come actually stay.

The Pharisees are like that invited guest who came but who was completely unresponsive to his host. On seeing the guest without the proper garment the host does not throw the man out. Rather he approaches him, calls him "friend," and asks him how he got in without a wedding garment.

Instead of responding to his host the guest is completely unresponsive. "And he was speechless" (Matthew 22:12). It is only at this point that the guest is thrown out.

The Pharisees are like this guest. They have been invited to the kingdom. From their point of view they have accepted the invitation. However, Jesus recognizes that they have come "improperly dressed," with the wrong disposition. He has come to them to help them, but they refuse to respond. They will not "remain at the marriage feast." They will not be in the kingdom.

Jesus had earlier taught this same lesson when he said, "It is not those who say to me, 'Lord, Lord,' who will enter the kingdom of heaven, but the person who does the will of my Father in heaven" (Matthew 7:21).

The Pharisees' reaction to Jesus' parable is to plot against him. Evidently Jesus' words challenged the Pharisees to the depth of their beings. Since they did not want to listen to his words and to change their way of life, to convert, they decided instead to destroy the one who kept confronting them.

When we look at this parable in the context of Jesus' conversation with the Pharisees we can see that the improperly dressed guest is not thrown out of the wedding feast through no fault of his own. Instead, he is thrown out because of his complete lack of response to the king who is willing to call him "friend." Through the parable Jesus is teaching the Pharisees that this same fate awaits them.

Review Questions

1. Of what does Jesus accuse the Pharisees through the parable of the two sons?
2. Of what does Jesus warn the Pharisees in the parable of the wicked tenants?
3. Of what does Jesus warn the Pharisees in the parable of the marriage feast?
4. How is this lesson drawn from the parable?

Discussion Questions

1. Do you think that you have been invited to the wedding feast?
2. What do you think it means that the servants gathered "bad and good alike" for the wedding feast?
3. What do you think it would take to be properly responsive to an invitation to the kingdom?

ARTICLE 17

Parables Are Not Allegories

Question: "Doesn't the parable of the talents (Matthew 25:14–39) give support to a profit motive in business practices? It seems that even God demands a profit." (Matthew 24:3; 25:1–13 also discussed)

One of the mistakes people often make when interpreting scripture is to bring a question to the scripture which is on one's mind and then to find an answer by taking a passage completely out of context. When one does this one is usually using scripture (or abusing scripture) to support an opinion one had before reading the scripture. This is called "proof texting." Proof texting is the opposite of allowing one's mind and heart to be formed by the living word.

The person who asked this question has made this mistake. The parable of the talents is not teaching anything at all about business practices. Rather, it is teaching something about the kingdom of God.

A second mistake which lies behind this question is that the person has not interpreted the parable as a parable. Instead the person has interpreted the parable as an allegory.

An allegory is a different literary form entirely. In an allegory there are two levels of meaning: a literal or surface level and an intentional level. Each of the details of the story on the surface level stands for something on the intentional level. The real point of the story lies on the intentional level.

As has been pointed out before, in a parable the comparison is not between the surface and intentional levels of the story but between one element in the story and the audience.

It is obvious that the person who asked this question has interpreted the parable as though it were an allegory because the person has said, "Even God demands a profit." Actually, God does not appear in this story. The person who demanded a profit was not God but the master who had servants and then went abroad. Only if one allegorizes the parable does that master stand for God.

Let us interpret this parable as a parable and see what lesson Jesus is teaching his audience.

The parable of the talents is part of Jesus' eschatological discourse, or his discourse about "end times." The discourse starts back in Chapter 24 when the disciples ask Jesus, "Tell us, when will this be, and what will be the sign of your coming and of the close of the age?" (Matthew 24:3).

In the next two chapters the collator of Matthew's gospel has arranged a number of inherited materials about the end times.

So Jesus is telling this parable to the disciples who have asked when the end times will come and what they should watch out for.

Preceding the parable of the talents is the parable of the ten bridesmaids (Matthew 25:1–13), five of whom forget to bring oil for their lamps and thus miss the coming of the bridegroom. In this parable Jesus teaches his disciples, who compare to the bridesmaids, that they should always be ready because they do not know when the end times will come.

Jesus then continues his teaching about the end times with the parable of the talents. In this parable the disciples compare to the servants who have been entrusted with a varying number of "talents." (The word refers to a coin but works well as a pun in English.) When the master returns he is pleased with the servant who was given five talents and now has ten. He is also pleased with the servant who was given two talents and now has four. However, the master is not pleased with the servant who had only one talent and buried it.

What is the root of this third servant's failure? We know the answer to this question because Jesus provides us with this information as he pictures the servant defending his action: "So I

INTERPRETING PARABLES AS PARABLES

A Parable: Look for one basic comparison between an element in the story and the audience listening to the story. The lesson comes from this comparison. Ask yourself:
- To whom is Jesus speaking?
- What's the topic?
- With what person or thing in the story does the audience compare?
- What lesson is drawn from this comparison?

Example: The Parable of the Talents (Matthew 25:14–39)

- Jesus is speaking to the disciples.
- Jesus is speaking about the end times.
- The disciples compare to the servants who have been given talents and are waiting for the return of the master.
- Jesus is teaching his disciples not to wait in fear for the "end time" or they will fail to accomplish anything while they wait.

An Allegory: Look for a second level of meaning by equating each element on the literal level with an element on the allegorical level.

TO INTERPRET THE PARABLE OF THE TALENTS AS AN
ALLEGORY IS TO MISUNDERSTAND IT

Example:
- The master stands for God.
- The servants stand for God's people.
- The talents stand for jobs.
- The profit on the investment of talents stands for profit in business.

- Lesson: "Even God demands a profit."

THIS LESSON IS INCOMPATIBLE WITH THE GOSPELS. THE
ROOT OF THE MISTAKE IS TO INTERPRET A PARABLE
AS THOUGH IT WERE AN ALLEGORY.

was afraid, and I went off and hid your talent in the ground"
(Matthew 25:24). Fear was the fault that defeated this servant.

Through this parable Jesus is not teaching anything about
business practices. Nor is Jesus saying that the master in the
story stands for God. Rather, Jesus is teaching his disciples not to
wait in fear for the "end times" or they will fail to accomplish
anything while they wait.

Review Questions

1. What is "proof texting"? Why is this not a good way to "use"
   scripture?
2. What is an allegory? How does it differ from a parable?
3. What is Jesus teaching his disciples through the parable of the
   ten bridesmaids?
4. What is Jesus teaching his disciples through the parable of the
   talents?

Discussion Questions

1. Do you take predictions about "the end of the world" seriously? Based on the parables discussed in this article, what do
   you think Jesus might say to a person upset by such a prediction?
2. Do you agree with the statement, "We have nothing to fear
   but fear itself"? How does this question relate to the parable
   of the talents?

ARTICLE 18

Covenant Celebrations

Question: "At the last supper when Jesus took the cup and said, 'This is my blood,' why did he make a point of calling it 'the blood of the covenant'?" (Matthew 26:28).

In order to understand why Jesus calls the cup "the blood of the covenant" one has to remember that Jesus and his apostles are celebrating the passover meal. The passover meal was (and is) celebrated each year in order to commemorate God's covenant with his people, and more specifically God's saving power at the time of the exodus. Jesus, in the midst of this covenant celebration, redefines the covenant and institutes a new way to celebrate a new covenant.

All of this will become clearer if we back up and review the idea of a covenant as well as the experience which resulted in the annual passover celebration.

There is hardly any concept that would have been more familiar to Matthew's Jewish audience than the idea of a covenant. For two thousand years, going all the way back to their father in faith, Abraham, the Jews had conceptualized their relationship with God as a covenant.

In Abraham's time a covenant was the most solemn of agreements and could never be broken. Abraham experienced God's power and presence in his life in such a way that he felt himself in a covenant relationship with God. God would give Abraham protection, land and descendants. Abraham would have faith in his God and obey him.

Six hundred years later the Hebrews still understand themselves to be in a covenant relationship with Yahweh. At this time

117

in their history, around 1250 B.C., the people had been the slaves of the Egyptians for four hundred years. In order to free his people, God raised up a great leader, Moses, who led the people out of slavery.

However, to leave Egypt was no easy matter. The Pharaoh did not want to let the people go, but he was finally forced to let the Hebrews leave because Egypt suffered a number of plagues, the worst of which resulted in the death of the Egyptian children. The plague killed the Egyptian children but not the Hebrew children. The fact that the Hebrew children were saved is at the root of the passover celebration. The Hebrews had put the blood of a slain lamb on their lintels and the "angel of death" had passed over their homes. This led to the Hebrews' escape, to the exodus, to their passing over from slavery to freedom.

With the passover celebration, then, the Jews are remembering this occasion on which the blood of the lamb saved their children and resulted in the people being freed from political slavery.

In the midst of celebrating God's saving power for his people, Jesus takes the wine of the passover celebration and identifies it with his blood. This blood will be poured out, not to free people from physical death or from political slavery, but to free them from eternal death, from slavery to sin. Thus Jesus identifies his blood as "the blood of the covenant, which is poured out for many for the forgiveness of sins" (Matthew 26:28).

By using the word "covenant," then, Jesus shows the apostles the relationship between their history, their present, and their future. He redefines the elements of the covenant in such a way that the apostles may understand what God is accomplishing for his people through Jesus' life and death. Jesus initiates a new covenant and a new table celebration to celebrate that covenant.

Every time we celebrate the eucharist we are celebrating the new covenant which God has established with his people, the church.

The word "testament" means "covenant." When we refer to the Hebrew scripture as the Old Testament and the Greek scripture as the New Testament we are once again referring to the fact that the word "covenant" has been used to conceptualize the relationship between God and his people for four thousand years. The word "covenant" is central to our understanding of the mutual and everlasting love which exists between God and his chosen people.

Review Questions

1. To what would the word "covenant" refer in the minds of Matthew's Jewish audience?
2. What do Jews celebrate on the feast of passover?
3. How might a Jew who lived before Jesus understand the words "the blood of the lamb which gives life"? How might a Christian understand those words?
4. What are we celebrating when we celebrate the eucharist?

Discussion Questions

1. For a religion to appropriate and redefine already existing celebrations is not unusual. Can you think of any other examples of this? (Why is Christmas on December 25? Why do we have Easter eggs?)
2. Is the word "covenant" a meaningful word to you to describe the special relationship between God and his people? Would another word or image be more meaningful for you? Why or why not?

Summation and Transition
from Matthew's to Luke's Gospel

As we move from Matthew's to Luke's gospel we can, once again, take with us many of the concepts we have learned.

All that was said about infancy narratives will be helpful in understanding Luke's infancy narrative.

In addition, our understanding of how the gospel collator molded materials to emphasize a particular theme for a particular audience will help us understand Luke. Luke's audience and purpose differ from Matthew's but he too molds inherited materials to meet the needs of an audience.

Our understanding that we must consider tone to determine meaning and that we must read passages in the context of the relationships in which they appear will also hold us in good stead.

To respond to several of the questions raised by Matthew's gospel we saw that we had to learn to hold biblical passages in tension with each other. Some statements which are true become untrue if one takes them as the whole truth and fails to balance them with other statements on the same subject (for example, statements on prayer and on the kingdom). We must learn to deal with paradox in order to understand the gospels.

All that we have learned about parable interpretation will be invaluable in understanding Luke. Some of our most memorable parables appear in Luke's gospel.

It is now time to read Luke's gospel. Once again, read the gospel as you would a novel so that you get a sense of the whole and a sense of how each part fits into the whole. As you read, jot down your questions. Many of the questions you ask will be discussed in the articles on Luke's gospel which follow.

■ THE GOSPEL ACCORDING ■
■ *to Luke* ■

ARTICLE 1

Dramatization: A Way To Teach
the Meaning of an Event

Question: "Is the description of the angel announcing Jesus' birth to Mary (Luke 1:26–38) a literal description of the event or a dramatization of an internal thought process?" (2 Corinthians 12:2–4 also discussed)

This question was obviously asked by a person who realizes that a gospel contains within it a variety of kinds of writing which have been collated by an editor. In studying Matthew's infancy narrative we learned that we should not read these stories which surround Jesus' birth as though they were primarily historical documents. They are not. They are primarily theological documents.

So while I would not want to describe the account of the annunciation to Mary as a literal description of an event, neither would I want to describe it as a dramatization of an internal thought process.

How one would respond to the question would be partly determined by the view of reality which one brings to the text. Is there an existing reality which is referred to by the word "angel"? Do "angels" exist? Or is the word "angel" a personification, a way of referring to an abstract concept rather than a way of referring to a spiritual being?

It is not unreasonable to believe that created spiritual beings, "angels," exist. When we look at the world around us and see all the gradations of beings which God has created in the material realm it seems very unlikely that there are no created beings between us and God. What a jump that would be! Traditionally, we have thought of gradations of spiritual beings and have referred to them as "choirs of angels."

If one admits the possibility that there are spiritual beings, then one probably does not read the account of the annunciation as a dramatization of an internal thought process. Such a person would consider "what happened" to have been an *interaction* between Mary and another, not an internal psychological process of Mary's.

However, to say this is not to say that the account of the annunciation is a realistic description of the experience which Mary had. We do not understand, nor do we have an accurate vocabulary to describe our interaction with those not living in bodies on earth as we are. If we have a deeply spiritual experience we don't understand it ourselves nor can we accurately describe it to another. Paul struggles with this problem when he describes an experience of his.

> I know a man in Christ who fourteen years ago was caught up to the third heaven—whether in the body or out of the body I do not know, God knows. And I know that this man was caught up into paradise—whether in the body or out of the body I do not know. God knows—and he heard things that cannot be told, which man may not utter (2 Corinthians 12:2–4).

Luke's account of the annunciation, unlike these words of Paul, is not an attempt to accurately describe the profound spiritual experience which Mary had, but to reveal the ramifications of the experience to his readers.

By using the technique of a simple dialogue between an angel and Mary, Luke places on Gabriel's lips the astounding truth.

> And behold you will conceive in your womb and bear a son, and you shall call his name Jesus. He will be great, and will be called the Son of the Most High; and the Lord God will give to him the throne of his father David, and he will reign over the house of Jacob forever; and of his kingdom there will be no end (Luke 1:31–33).

In terms of narrative, then, the account is a dramatization but not a dramatization of an internal psychological process. Rather, it is a dramatization of an indescribable spiritual interaction between God or God's messenger and a simple maiden chosen to be the mother of God.

Review Questions

1. Is the account of the annunciation primarily an example of historical writing? Explain.
2. To what does the phrase "choirs of angels" refer?
3. From a narrative point of view (i.e. the way the story is told) what is the difference in purpose between Paul's account of his experience in 2 Corinthians 12:2–4 and Luke's account of Mary's experience at the annunciation?
4. Through the story of the annunciation what is Luke teaching his audience?

Discussion Questions

1. Why is it true to say that decisions about literary form are influenced by the view of reality which one brings to the text?
2. Do you believe in the existence of angels? Why or why not?
3. Why is it difficult, if not impossible, to give an accurate description of a deeply spiritual experience?

ARTICLE 2

Luke's Infancy Narrative:
Interpreting Images

Question: "What is the significance behind Luke's saying, 'And she gave birth to her first-born son and wrapped him in swaddling clothes and laid him in a manger, because there was no place for them in the inn' (Luke 2:7)? I gather there is more here than meets the eye." (Colossians 1:15–16; Wisdom 7:1–6 also discussed)

Once again we see that the person who asked this question understands that a variety of literary forms appear in a gospel. We can tell that the questioner understands this because she recognizes the possibility that there is more in Luke's account than a straightforward description of events. And she is right.

We are on the right track if we start with the presumption that the question behind the infancy narratives is not simply "What happened?" but "What is the significance of what happened?"

Luke's account, as did Matthew's, weaves images throughout the account of events in order to make clear to his audience the significance of those events.

Again, our task is to understand the images.

Mary's son was her "first-born." By the time Luke was addressing his Gentile audience (85 A.D.) the hymn which we read in Colossians would have been well known.

> He is the image of the invisible God, the first-born of all creation: for in him all things were created, in heaven and on earth (Colossians 1:15–16).

The word "first-born" had come to be a reference to the post-resurrection understanding of Christ in his cosmic role as first in

---

POINTS FOUND ONLY IN LUKE'S ACCOUNT

- The annunciation to Mary
- The story of Elizabeth, Zechariah, and the birth of John the Baptist
- The census which brings Joseph and Mary to Bethlehem
- Jesus wrapped in swaddling clothes and placed in the manger
- The announcement of Jesus' birth to the shepherds
- The presentation of Jesus in the temple and the response of Simeon and Anna
- Jesus lost and later found in the temple when he was a young boy

---

the order of creation and first to rise from the dead. (See Hebrews 1:4–14 and Revelation 1:4–6 for more evidence of the meaning of "first-born.")

But Luke is preaching not just a God, but a God become man. This is the meaning behind "swaddling clothes."

> Like all the others, I too am a mortal man. . . .
> I was nurtured in swaddling clothes, with every care.
> (See Wisdom 7:1–6—Jerusalem Bible)

The "first-born" in "swaddling clothes" is both divine and human.

Luke does not place Jesus in an inn because an inn is a place where travelers stay for a night. Jesus has come not just to visit but to dwell with his people and become their source of life.

A manger is the place where the food for the flock is placed. Jesus is food for the flock, so he is placed in the manger. (John's gospel teaches us this truth when he has Jesus say, "I am the bread of life.")

When Jesus was alive on earth his followers did not recognize him. However, after the resurrection, and by the time the infancy narratives were taking form, Christ's followers did recog-

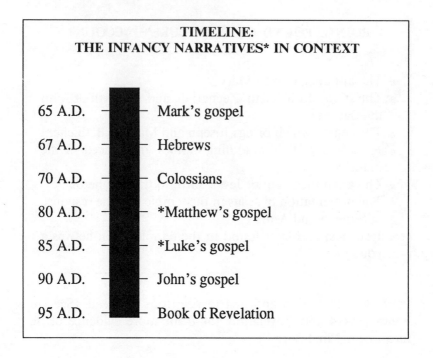

TIMELINE:
THE INFANCY NARRATIVES* IN CONTEXT

65 A.D.	Mark's gospel
67 A.D.	Hebrews
70 A.D.	Colossians
80 A.D.	*Matthew's gospel
85 A.D.	*Luke's gospel
90 A.D.	John's gospel
95 A.D.	Book of Revelation

nize their Lord. The leaders of the church, the shepherds, did recognize the food for their flock.

This is why Luke pictures the angels announcing the birth of the child to the shepherds and the shepherds believing and rushing to Bethlehem to see the baby lying in the manger. Luke's apparently simple images of the babe in the manger greeted by shepherds are Luke's way of announcing to his Gentile audience that the baby Jesus, the risen Lord, is now recognized as both God and man, the source of life for his people.

Review Questions

1. What presumption should we bring to the infancy narratives?
2. What would the word "first-born" have meant to Luke's audience of 85 A.D.?
3. To what would the phrase "swaddling clothes" have referred?

What truth about Jesus' identity was being taught through this allusion?

4. Why is Jesus not pictured in an inn?
5. Why is Jesus pictured in a manger?
6. What is symbolized by the shepherds' recognition of Jesus?

Discussion Questions

1. Now that you understand how to interpret the infancy narratives do you treasure them all the more or do you feel as though you have lost something? Explain.
2. Do you think of God as an occasional visitor or as one who dwells with his people? Explain.
3. What does it mean to say that Jesus is nourishment for his people?

ARTICLE 3

Who Can Forgive Sin?

Question: "Why did Jesus ask, 'Which is easier to say, "Your sins are forgiven you," or to say, "Rise and walk"?' This seems like a strange question." (Luke 5:23; 5:17–25 also included.)

This does seem like a strange question. Why? Because the question seems a little stupid, a little off the subject—as though Jesus has lost the drift of the conversation.

Since we are contextualists, people who read scripture passages in context, we must put Jesus' words in the context in which they appear in Luke's gospel. To whom is Jesus speaking? What is Jesus' relationship with his audience?

Jesus asks this question of the Pharisees who are witnessing and criticizing Jesus' interaction with a paralytic whose friends had lowered him through the roof in order to ask Jesus to heal him. Jesus' first words to the man were, "Your sins are forgiven you" (Luke 5:20).

Put yourself in the place of that man for just a moment. How do you think he felt? If you were paralyzed and your friends brought you before Jesus in order to ask for a healing, would you be pleased to hear, "Your sins are forgiven you"? Even though spiritual healing is by far the more important healing, it is not the healing the man wanted. Why did Jesus say this? Usually he asks a person what he or she wants.

Jesus said this in order to get exactly the reaction he did get from the Pharisees who are watching and waiting to criticize. "And the scribes and Pharisees began to question, saying, 'Who is this that speaks blasphemies? Who can forgive sins but God only?' " (Luke 5:21).

130

It is at this point that Jesus asks the question, "Which is easier to say, 'Your sins are forgiven you,' or 'Rise and walk'?"

The question in the mind of the Pharisees is not: "Which is easier to say?" Anyone can *say* either. The question is, "Is there any power behind the words? Who is Jesus to forgive sins?" The Pharisees think that Jesus' words must be empty words—words with no effect.

However, Jesus' words are not empty words. Jesus' words are effective. One cannot see sin forgiven, but one can see paralysis healed. And in the Pharisees' mind there is a connection between the two. They think of sickness as being a punishment for sin.

When Jesus asks a question that seems a little dim-witted and off the subject he is using Socratic irony. He is asking a question, not because he wants to learn the answer but because he wants to spur the thinking of the person to whom the question is addressed.

Jesus is well aware of the Pharisees' doubts about him. So, after highlighting their doubts with his Socratic irony, Jesus gets to the point. " 'But that you may know that the Son of Man has authority on earth to forgive sins'—he said to the man who was paralyzed—'I say to you, rise, take up your bed and go home.' And immediately he rose before them, and took up that on which he lay, and went home, glorifying God. And amazement seized them all, and they glorified God and were filled with awe, saying, 'We have seen strange things today' " (Luke 5:24–26).

Indeed, the Pharisees must have been amazed. Who was this "Son of Man" who healed? Could he also forgive sins? The Pharisees are left with questions rather than answers.

Students sometimes interpret the words "glorified God" as meaning "glorified Jesus." Since the student believes Jesus is God, he or she may not realize that Jesus' contemporaries did not have this understanding. Jesus' contemporaries certainly did not think of Jesus as divine. Jesus' divinity was a post-resurrection insight, one which Luke shares with his Gentile audience of 85 A.D., but not one which Luke pictures Jesus' contemporaries as having. So in addition to showing Jesus using Socratic irony,

Luke is using dramatic irony. He, his original audience, and we all know that Jesus can forgive sins because he is God become man. Jesus' contemporaries do not know this, but in this scene we see them confronted with the question: "Who is the Son of Man if he can forgive sins?"

Review Questions

1. What is a contextualist?
2. Why did the Pharisees think that Jesus' words were blasphemous?
3. What is Socratic irony? Why does Jesus use Socratic irony?
4. After the healing, when those present glorified God, were they glorifying Jesus? Explain.

Discussion Questions

1. Do you think people still tend to regard sickness or ill fortune as a punishment from God? Why or why not?
2. Which do you think is more important, physical or spiritual health? Which would you rather have? Which does your prayer life reflect that you would rather have?
3. To whom does the power to forgive sin belong? Is forgiveness of sin accessible to you? How? Is forgiveness of sin visible in any way? How?

ARTICLE 4

God Loves First

Question: "I always thought that Jesus told the woman who washed his feet at Simon's house, 'Because you have loved much you have been forgiven much.' Now that I read her words in context it seems that Jesus is actually saying, 'Because you have been forgiven much you love much.' Which is it?" (Luke 7:36–50)

Jesus' words, as they appear in the Revised Standard Version, are "Therefore I tell you, her sins, which are many, are forgiven, for she loved much" (Luke 7:47). The "for" in the quotation could be understood to mean "*because* she loved much" or "*as evidenced by the fact* that she loved much." In other words, the word "for" could mean that the woman's love is the reason she has been forgiven much, or it could mean that her love is the evidence that she has been forgiven much. In order to answer the question and see which of these two interpretations is correct we need to put the words in context.

Jesus is having dinner at the house of a Pharisee named Simon (no relation to Simon Peter). A woman who is a sinner comes to Jesus, "and standing behind him at his feet, weeping, she began to wet his feet with her tears, and wiped them with the hair of her head, and kissed his feet, and anointed them with the ointment" (Luke 7:38).

Imagine, just for a moment, that you had also been a guest in the same home that evening. How do you think you would have felt toward the woman? Remember also that she was showing a great deal of love and reverence toward Jesus, which he, evidently, was accepting. Do you think you would have felt any sympathy for the woman?

Simon didn't. Simon already had the woman categorized in his mind. "This woman is a sinner and you'd think Jesus wouldn't want to be seen being touched by a woman like this." How, one wonders, did Simon know the woman was a sinner? Surely Simon isn't a sinner himself?

Obviously, Simon does not think of himself as a sinner. He thinks of himself as far superior to the woman. Simon thinks that there is no reason why Jesus should not want to be seen with him, a proper citizen.

Jesus realizes that Simon considers himself morally superior to the woman. In order to point this out to Simon, as well as to suggest that Simon might be wrong in his assessment, Jesus tells Simon the parable of the two debtors (see Luke 7:41–42). Two debtors are both forgiven, one who owes a large amount and one who owes less. Jesus then asks Simon, "Which of them (the debtors) will love him more?" (Luke 7:42).

As in all parables, the lesson which Jesus is teaching his audience is discovered by asking, "To whom in the story does Jesus' audience compare?" Simon compares to the debtor who has been forgiven little. The woman, on the other hand, compares to the debtor who has been forgiven much. Jesus is telling Simon that the woman, by the fact that she loves much, reveals that she has already experienced God's forgiveness. The experience of having been forgiven lies at the root of her ability to have and express such love.

Simon, on the other hand, is self-righteous. Simon does not see himself as a sinner and so he has no sense of having been forgiven. His self-righteous posture has left him less able to love others—both Jesus and the woman.

Jesus is telling Simon the answer to our original question about the woman—her great love is the evidence that she has already been forgiven, not the reason she has been forgiven. In the spiritual life God takes the initiative and loves us first. We don't earn God's love; we respond to it.

In addition, Jesus is telling Simon something about himself. Simon's self-righteous attitude is preventing him from experiencing God's love and from loving others. Although Simon doesn't know it, the woman is better off, spiritually, than he is.

Review Questions

1. What two meanings might the word "for" have in "for she loved much"?
2. What fault in himself does Simon reveal by his reaction to the woman?
3. In the parable, which comes first: forgiveness or love?
4. Which of the two possible meanings of "for" fits the context?

Discussion Questions

1. If you had also been a guest in Simon's house, how do you think you would have responded toward the penitent woman?
2. Why are a sense of superiority and a judgmental attitude blocks to spiritual growth?
3. Do you think you earn God's love? Why or why not?

ARTICLE 5

Mary in the Synoptic Gospels

Question: "Why would Jesus ignore and insult Mary? When Jesus is told that his mother and brothers are standing outside and want to see him, Jesus says, 'My mother and my brothers are those who hear the word of God and do it' " (Luke 8:21; Mark 6:3; 3:20–21; 3:31–34; Matthew 12:46–50; Luke 1:38; 4:22; 11:27–28 also discussed)

For people who have a love for and devotion to Mary, the way Mary is pictured in the synoptic gospels comes as quite a surprise. Were it not for the infancy narratives we would know next to nothing about Jesus' mother. In Luke's gospel, the passage in question is the only passage, outside of the infancy narratives, in which Mary is even mentioned.

The infancy narratives, as we already know, are late developments. Evidently the very early gospel material did not reflect a particular interest in or respect for Mary.

The passage in question appears, with slight variations, in each of the synoptic gospels. While the words in each account are similar, their context in their respective gospels gives the words a very different meaning from one gospel to the next.

In Mark's gospel we read, "And his mother and his brothers came; and standing outside they sent to him and called him. And a crowd was sitting about him, and they said to him, 'Your mother and your brothers are outside asking for you.' And he replied, 'Who are my mother and my brothers?' And looking around on those who sat about him, he said, 'Here are my mother and my brothers! Whoever does the will of God is my brother, and sister, and mother' " (Mark 3:31–34).

136

**PASSAGES IN WHICH MARY IS NAMED
IN THE SYNOPTIC GOSPELS**

In Mark
6:3

In Matthew
1:16–1:20
2:11
13:55

In Luke
1:27–1:56
2:5
2:16
2:19
2:34

(They are nearly all in the birth narratives.)

This account in Mark's gospel does seem to dismiss Mary and Jesus' "brothers" (a word with a more precise meaning in English than it would have had in Greek, *koine,* the language in which Luke's gospel was originally written; to Luke's audience the word could have meant "brother," "cousin," "relative," or "follower"). Jesus specifically looks around at the crowd and calls *them* "brother, sister and mother." Since there is no infancy narrative in Mark we have no larger context within which to put this passage.

To make matters worse, an earlier reference to Jesus' family is also unflattering: "Then he went home, and the crowd came together again, so that they could not even eat. And when his family heard it, they went out to seize him, for people were saying, 'He is beside himself' " (Mark 3:20–21).

Mark's gospel seems to reflect not only a lack of interest in but a certain antagonism toward Mary. Could this be because Mary was thought by her contemporaries to have conceived a child before she was married? Did Mary suffer from people's scorn? Was Jesus thought to be illegitimate?

Later in Mark's gospel Jesus is pictured as returning to his home country to teach in the synagogue. The people exclaim, "Is not this the carpenter, the son of Mary?" (Mark 6:3). There is no reference to Joseph. Nor does Mark's gospel include a genealogy.

It is this picture of Mary that Luke inherited in his source, Mark. But similar words have an entirely different meaning in Luke because of their context.

In Luke we read the beautiful story of the annunciation to Mary. We know that Mary is a virtuous person and one totally open to God. With complete trust Mary says, "Behold, I am the handmaid of the Lord: let it be to me according to your word" (Luke 1:38).

Mary, full of grace, is still fresh in our minds as Jesus makes his comment. When we hear Jesus say that his mother and brothers are those who hear the word of God and do it, we do not hear this as a contrasting statement excluding Mary. The words describe Mary. They are a compliment to her, for she has always heard God's word and done it. Notice that Jesus does not point to someone else—the crowd, as he did in Mark, or the disciples, as he did in Matthew (see Matthew 12:46–50). Luke has omitted any gesture that would allow Jesus' words to refer to anyone but his family.

The fact that Mary was open to and obedient to God's word was more important than that she was, biologically, Jesus' mother. Jesus himself acknowledges this when he responds to the woman who said, "Blessed is the womb that bore you, and the breasts that you sucked." "But he said, 'Blessed rather are those who hear the word of God and keep it' " (Luke 11:27–28).

Mary's greatest blessing is not in her biological relationship to Jesus but in her holiness. Mary is truly full of grace.

Luke, realizing this, treats Mary with every respect. When Jesus' parentage is referred to in Luke's gospel the people ask, "Is not this Joseph's son?" (Luke 4:22). Nowhere in Luke's gospel do we get a hint of lack of respect for Mary, the mother of Jesus.

Review Questions

1. If we had no infancy narratives, what would we know about Mary from the synoptic gospels?
2. Why does the infancy narrative change the context of the words "My mother and my brothers are those who hear the word of God and do it" in Luke's gospel?
3. In addition to a changed context, how else does Luke alter his source, Mark?
4. What is the difference in meaning in these words in Luke and Mark?

Discussion Questions

1. If you had lived in Mary's town when Jesus was conceived, what conclusions do you think you would have drawn about her?
2. Why do you think interest in Mary was a later development?
3. What do you consider Mary's greatest blessing? Why?

ARTICLE 6

Jesus and "Women's Role"

Question: "Why did the woman with the flow of blood not ask Jesus for a healing the way others do? Why was she so hesitant to admit that she had touched Jesus' garment?" (Luke 8:42–48; 10:38–42 also discussed)

The woman with the flow of blood acted as she did because her condition made her unclean in her society. For her to touch another person would have been to make that person ritually unclean.

The book of Leviticus details the degree to which this woman with the flow of blood would have been ostracized by her society: "Whenever a woman has a discharge and the discharge from her body is of blood, she will remain in a state of menstrual pollution for seven days. Anyone who touches her will be unclean until evening" (Leviticus 15:19). "If a woman has a prolonged discharge of blood outside the period, or if the period is prolonged, during the time the discharge lasts she will be in the same state of uncleanness as during her monthly periods" (Leviticus 15:25).

This poor woman, having suffered from the flow of blood for twelve years, would have spent all of those years as an outcast, on the fringe of society and isolated from a normal life. It took great courage for the woman to admit to Jesus and the others in the crowd what she had done.

Jesus felt nothing but love and compassion for the woman. He evidently wasn't worried about his ritual purity because he never mentioned it.

To an American reader the fact that the story shows Jesus' lack of concern about ritual cleanliness is missed. However, given the position of women in Jesus' society, his behavior

140

would have been extraordinary to a contemporary. Here was a man who did not let the laws force him to abandon or marginalize women. He ignored the question of ritual uncleanliness entirely.

This occasion is not the only one on which Luke pictures Jesus as acting in a completely unexpected way toward women. The same lack of conformity to the expectations of his society is evident when Jesus visits Martha and Mary. Martha welcomed Jesus into her home and treated him as a Jewish woman would have been expected to treat a man. She waited on him. Mary, on the other hand, acted in a completely unconventional way. She "sat at the Lord's feet and listened to his teaching" (Luke 10:39). Once again, Jesus accepts the unconventional behavior of a woman without comment.

As is often true in today's world, the criticism of the woman who acts differently than society expects or demands comes from the woman who has accepted her more limited role without question. Martha complains to Jesus, "Lord, do you not care that my sister has left me to serve alone? Tell her then to help me" (Luke 10:40).

Many a generation of women have felt resentment at Jesus' response to Martha. "Martha, Martha, you are anxious and troubled about many things. One thing is needful. Mary has chosen the good portion, which shall not be taken away from her" (Luke 10:41).

Why have women resented these words? Because they think Jesus should have told Mary to help. After all, someone has to do the work.

It is true that work needs to be done. It is not true that such work is always the highest priority and should take precedence over other things, such as spending time listening and learning, spending time giving full attention to a loved one.

The idea that a woman would choose to sit at Jesus' feet and learn, rather than knowing that her place was to wait on him, would have been jarring to Luke's audience.

Once again Luke shows Jesus accepting completely unconventional and unexpected behavior on the part of a woman and thus challenging the laws and conventions of his society which have marginalized or limited those women.

Review Questions

1. Why did it take courage for the woman with the flow of blood to admit what she had done?
2. What was unconventional about Mary's behavior when Jesus visited Martha and Mary?
3. What does Jesus' behavior toward these women say about the laws and conventions which have marginalized them?

Discussion Questions

1. The woman with the flow of blood violated the laws of her society to get help. Can you think of situations in our society where similar action might be necessary?
2. When you hear the story of Martha and Mary do you side with one or the other? Which one? Why?
3. As you read the interpretation of these two incidents, what did you feel? Pleased? Annoyed? Do you know why you reacted as you did?

ARTICLE 7

Luke's Theme and Structure

Question: "Luke seems to give a different picture of Jesus' relationship with the disciples than Mark did. Is this true?" (Luke 9:45; 10:23–24; 22:3–4; 22:30–32; 22:45; Mark 8:14–21; 8:27–33)

In Luke's account of Jesus' sermon on the plain we hear Jesus teach, "Judge not, and you will not be judged; condemn not, and you will not be condemned; forgive, and you will be forgiven" (Luke 6:37). Luke seems to have truly taken these words to heart as he tells the story of the disciples' behavior during Jesus' public ministry and during his passion, death and resurrection.

Luke seems to bend over backward to refrain from judging the disciples when they fail. He omits several accounts which are in Mark, Luke's source, and which cast an unfavorable light on the disciples. He specifically shows Jesus praising and complimenting the disciples for their success in a way not present in Mark. When Luke must tell of failures on the part of the disciples he does his best to put the kindest interpretation possible on their actions.

Surely two of the episodes in Mark's gospel which make the difficult relationship between Jesus and his disciples painfully obvious are the time when they take Jesus' warning, "Beware of the yeast of the Pharisees," as a reminder that they have forgotten to bring any bread (Mark 8:14–21), and the time when Jesus rebukes Peter, calling Peter "Satan" (Mark 8:27–33). Even though Mark is one of Luke's sources, Luke omits each of these episodes.

143

THE GOSPEL ACCORDING TO LUKE	
Date	85 A.D.
Audience	Gentiles
Sources	Mark; "Q"; "L"
Organization	An infancy narrative A geographic organization: Jesus has a Galilean ministry, a trip to Jerusalem, and a Jerusalem ministry An account of the passion, death and resurrection
Theme	The covenant relationship is universal
Goes back to . . .	A genealogy to Adam

In addition to leaving out various episodes, Luke shows the disciples experiencing success and Jesus affirming the disciples in a way not present in Mark. In Luke's account the seventy-two return jubilant at their success and Jesus praises them. "Then turning to the disciples he said privately, 'Blessed are the eyes which see what you see! For I tell you that many prophets and kings desired to see what you see, and did not see it, and to hear what you hear, and did not hear it' " (Luke 10:23–24).

Even at the last supper, just before Jesus warns Peter that he will betray him, Jesus speaks words of praise to his disciples. "You are those who have continued with me in my trials, and I assign to you, as my Father assigned to me, a kingdom, that you may eat and drink at my table in my kingdom, and sit on thrones judging the twelve tribes of Israel" (Luke 22:30).

Even when Luke cannot avoid putting the disciples in a bad light because they do betray, deny and desert Jesus, nevertheless Luke puts the kindest interpretation possible on their actions.

When Luke must describe Judas' and Peter's behavior he attributes it to Satan: "Then Satan entered into Judas called Iscariot, who was of the number of the twelve; he went away and conferred with the chief priests and officers how he might betray him to them" (Luke 22:3–4).

When Jesus warns Peter of his coming betrayal Luke pictures Jesus as saying, "Simon, Simon, behold, Satan demanded to have you, that he might sift you like wheat, but I have prayed for you that your faith may not fail; and when you have turned again, strengthen your brethren" (Luke 22:31–33).

When the disciples fall asleep in the garden of Gethsemane, Luke does not dwell on their failure, showing Jesus coming to find the disciples asleep three times. Luke mentions it only once and says, "He (Jesus) came to the disciples and found them sleeping from sorrow" (Luke 22:45).

All through Luke's gospel we see Luke refusing to place the responsibility for failing to understand at the feet of the disciples themselves. When the disciples fail to understand Luke says, "It was concealed from them, that they should not perceive it" (Luke 9:45).

Although some of these details can be attributed to the fact that Luke himself must have been a kind-hearted, non-judgmental person, their importance goes deeper than a personality characteristic of the editor. These details reflect Luke's understanding about "the coming of the kingdom." Luke is writing to a Gentile audience, probably in Ephesus, who, after two thousand years, had been included in the covenant. They had not rejected Yahweh up till now. The truth had been hidden from them. Now their time had come. Luke seems to have a deep sense that all is happening in God's time, one step at a time.

This sense of an orderly progression is evident even in Luke's structure. Rather than being organized thematically, as was Matthew's gospel, Luke's gospel is organized geographically. Jesus has a Galilean ministry, then goes on a journey to Jerusalem, and then has a Jerusalem ministry. This same geographic organization is present in the second volume of Luke's work, the Acts of the Apostles.

MARK, MATTHEW, AND LUKE'S GOSPELS

	Mark	Matthew	Luke
Date	65 A.D.	80 A.D.	85 A.D.
Audience	Persecuted Christians	Settled Jewish Christians	Gentiles
Sources	The inherited oral and written traditions of the believing community	Mark "Q" "M"	Mark "Q" "L"
Organization	The passion, death and resurrection preceded by some miracle stories and some controversies with the Pharisees	An infancy narrative; five thematic sections each containing a narrative and a speech by Jesus; an account of the passion, death, and resurrection	An infancy narrative; a geographic organization: Jesus has a Galilean ministry, a trip to Jerusalem, and a Jerusalem ministry; an account of the passion, death, and resurrection.
Theme	"Why would anyone suffer?" Look to Christ and see that suffering leads to resurrection	Jesus is the new Moses with authority from God to give the new law	The covenant relationship is universal
Goes back to	The baptism of Jesus	A genealogy to Abraham	A genealogy to Adam

No wonder Luke refrains from judging the disciples. Luke sees them too as on a spiritual journey, and one which can be taken only one step at a time.

Review Questions

1. What unfavorable pictures of the disciples does Luke omit?
2. Name some occasions on which Luke pictures Jesus as praising the disciples.
3. Name some occasions on which Luke puts a kind interpretation on the disciples' failures.
4. What understanding about the coming of the kingdom is reflected in Luke's kind, non-judgmental attitude?
5. How is this understanding reflected in the structure of Luke's gospel?

Discussion Questions

1. A difference in emphasis in the gospels reflects a difference in audience. Why is Luke's emphasis more appropriate than was Mark's for Luke's Gentile audience?
2. When you see others who lack understanding do you feel judgmental toward them? Why or why not?
3. Do you have the same priorities in life and the same beliefs now that you had ten years ago? Explain. If the answer is "no," do you blame yourself for your earlier understanding? Why or why not? Do you think Luke would blame you? Why or why not?

ARTICLE 8

Parables: A Challenge to Conversion

Question: "Why won't Jesus answer the lawyer who asks, 'Who is my neighbor?' Instead he tells the story of the good Samaritan." (Luke 10:25–37)

Jesus does answer the lawyer's question. The parable is the answer. Jesus answers by telling a parable because the answer is one which the lawyer will not like and will resist. Remember, Jesus often uses parables to challenge a resistant audience that have "eyes but do not see, ears but do not hear."

Let's look at the whole conversation so that we can see how the parable answers the question, "Who is my neighbor?" The conversation begins with the lawyer asking Jesus, "What shall I do to inherit eternal life?"

However, this is not an innocent question. Luke tells us that the lawyer asked the question to "test" Jesus (Luke 10:25). Jesus immediately recognizes that the lawyer is not asking the question in order to learn. So Jesus as much as says, "You're a lawyer. You tell me."

At this invitation the lawyer can't resist giving a perfect answer. "You will love the Lord your God with all your heart, and with all your soul, and with all your strength, and with all your mind; and your neighbor as yourself" (Luke 10:27). Jesus can find nothing to add to this answer.

Now the lawyer feels foolish. If he already knew the answer, why did he ask the question? That is why Luke tells us that the next question is asked "to justify himself" (Luke 10:29). "And who is my neighbor?"

With this question the lawyer has inadvertently asked a ques-

148

tion to which he actually does not know the answer. The lawyer is unaware of his blindness and will resist the answer he gets.

Jesus then tells the story of a man, presumably a Jew, who is left half-dead in a ditch. A priest and a Levite, both upright citizens, good people like the lawyer, pass by without helping.

Next a Samaritan comes along. A Samaritan is the one person in the story with whom the lawyer would not be able to identify. Samaritans were despised as half-breeds. Samaritans were unclean. A good Jew could ignore a Samaritan and feel completely justified. However, this Samaritan overcomes the mutual hatred between Samaritans and Jews and helps the man in the ditch. Not only does he help him but he takes responsibility for his welfare. He plans to return and pay for whatever care the man has needed.

After telling the story Jesus asks the lawyer, "Which of these three, do you think, proved neighbor to the man who fell among the robbers?" (Luke 10:36). Notice the question is slightly altered from the lawyer's—not "Who is my neighbor?" but "Who acted as neighbor?"

The lawyer is very smart. He can see where this conversation is going. Since he hates the Samaritan so much he can't bring himself to say, "The Samaritan acted as neighbor." Instead he says, "The one who showed mercy to him" (Luke 10:37).

Jesus responds, "Go and do likewise" (Luke 10:37). However, the message is not just, "Go and help others in need." The message is, "Go and learn to love those your law allows you to neglect, as the Samaritan did. Overcome these racial hatreds and realize that the Samaritan is also your neighbor."

Once more we see that the parables are not pleasant stories to entertain. Rather they are stories directed at a specific audience, designed to challenge and call to conversion. Often the parable surfaces some fault in the listener to which the listener is totally blind. This lawyer had no idea that his strict observance of the law was blinding him to the truths which Jesus had to teach. Through the parable of the good Samaritan Jesus was able at least to raise the lawyer's awareness. However, that does not mean that the lawyer accepted Jesus' teaching and had a change of heart. Luke does not tell us if the lawyer ever overcame his resistance.

Review Questions

1. Why does Jesus answer the lawyer's question by telling him a parable?
2. What motive does the lawyer have when he asks, "What shall I do to inherit eternal life?"
3. What motive does the lawyer have when he asks, "Who is my neighbor?"
4. What is the lawyer's attitude toward Samaritans?
5. What is Jesus teaching the lawyer through the parable?

Discussion Questions

1. If Jesus were telling this parable to a lawyer in our society, who do you think might have the role of the Samaritan? Why?
2. Do you see areas in our society in which people seem to be blind and deaf to the gospel message? What are they?

ARTICLE 9

Holiness: Not for Sale

Question: "Why does Jesus tell the Pharisees that everything will be clean for them if they give alms? Is this true?" (Luke 11:41; Luke 22:35–38; 22:50 also discussed)

No, it is not true. No one can buy holiness. The words which prompted this question are these words of Jesus' to the Pharisees: "But rather give alms from what you have and indeed everything is clean for you" (Luke 11:41—Jerusalem Bible translation).

This sentence has obviously caused translators a problem. Why? Because the literal meaning of the words contradicts the rest of the paragraph in which the words appear. In order to solve the problem some translators have tried to reflect the intent of the words rather than the literal meaning of the words. For example, the RSV translates the sentence: "But give for alms those things which are within; and behold, everything is clean for you" (Luke 11:41).

The problem with such a solution is that the translators, in choosing to go for the intent of the words, change the tone. In changing the tone they may remain faithful to the teaching but not to the teacher. By changing the tone they change the picture we get of Jesus' personality.

Let us back up and look at the quotation in its context to see why the problem exists.

Jesus has been invited to dine with a Pharisee. Jesus goes in and sits down at the table without first washing. The Pharisee is astounded that Jesus would disobey the laws for ritual cleanliness in this way. It is just this kind of judgmental attitude and

151

legalistic thinking which Jesus finds wrong in the Pharisees. It is this attitude that results in the Pharisees' being so self-righteous and unloving, a real spiritual block.

So Jesus tells the Pharisees, "Now you Pharisees cleanse the outside of the cup and of the dish, but inside you are full of extortion and wickedness" (Luke 11:39). Jesus is angry because the Pharisees think they can become holy through performing external actions rather than through a conversion of heart.

Next Jesus speaks ironically. When Jesus says, "But rather give alms from what you have and all is clean for you" (Luke 11:41), he means, "Instead of converting in your heart ('But rather') you think that if you give alms everything will be clean for you. But you are wrong."

Jesus then continues, "But woe to you Pharisees! For you tithe mint and rue and every herb, and neglect justice and the love of God" (Luke 11:42). To tithe mint and rue is to be scrupulous about the tithe. The tithing law, to give ten percent of one's produce, applied to major crops, not to garden spices. The Pharisees did more than the law demanded on externals but ignored what is most important, their internal dispositions.

So to translate the line in question, "But give for alms those things which are within," is to remain faithful to Jesus' intent but to take out the irony. Is this a good idea?

Jesus seems to have used irony quite often. To translate out the irony is to give a different picture of Jesus' personality than the synoptic gospels give us and perhaps to blind us to the many other instances of irony which appear on Jesus' lips.

For instance, when Jesus and his disciples are at the last supper we read the following: " 'When I sent you out with no purse or bag or sandals, did you lack anything?' They said, 'Nothing.' He said to them, 'But now, let him who has a purse take it, and likewise a bag. And let him who has no sword sell his mantle and buy one. For I tell you that this scripture must be fulfilled in me. "And he was reckoned with transgressors": for what is written about me has its fulfillment.' And they said, 'Look, Lord, here are two swords.' And he said to them, 'It is enough' " (Luke 22:35–38).

Now, if we think of Jesus as a person who often slips into irony we see a very different meaning in these words than we see if we think of Jesus as not using irony. Did Jesus change all his instructions as he left his disciples? Did Jesus say that two swords would be sufficient? Or was Jesus fearing that the disciples would ignore all his instructions when they met with trouble? And was Jesus totally exasperated when the disciples continued to misunderstand him? Surely Jesus did not want to be defended with swords. He demonstrated this by healing the ear of the high priest's servant (Luke 22:50). The tone for "It is enough" is undoubtedly exasperation. Jesus is fed up (that's enough!) because his disciples once again failed to understand what he was saying to them.

It is important to understand that holiness cannot be bought, even with a tithe. It is also important to know that Jesus is often pictured as speaking ironically. Otherwise we, like the disciples, will simply misunderstand what Jesus is saying.

Review Questions

1. What behavior on Jesus' part annoyed the Pharisees?
2. What behavior on the Pharisees' part caused Jesus to criticize them?
3. How do we know that the tone of, "But rather, give alms from what you have and indeed everything is clean for you," is ironic?
4. Why is it important to realize that Jesus often speaks ironically?
5. Did Jesus want his disciples to take up swords? How do you know?

Discussion Questions

1. Do you think that by making financial contributions to worthy causes you can buy holiness? Why or why not?
2. What is the difference between almsgiving and buying holiness?
3. Do you think Jesus wants his followers to "take up swords"? On what do you base your opinion?

ARTICLE 10

Kingdom: Present or Future?

Question: "What is the kingdom? Sometimes Jesus talks about it as if it is already present (Luke 17:21), and sometimes he talks about it as a future event (Luke 12:56). Which is it?" (Luke 19:11–27)

It is true that we enter the world of paradox when we talk about the kingdom. A paradox exists when two statements which appear to be inconsistent with each other are both true. The questioner is correct in observing that the kingdom seems to be both a present and a future reality. Are these two ideas compatible? Let's look at the two passages in question and see.

First, the kingdom seems to be something which Jesus refers to as already present: "Being asked by the Pharisees when the kingdom of God was coming, he answered them, 'The kingdom of God is not coming with signs to be observed; nor will they say, "Lo, here it is!" or "There!" for behold, the kingdom of God is in the midst of you' " (Luke 17:20–21).

Notice that when Jesus says this, he is speaking to the Pharisees. The Pharisees, as we already know, are prone to concentrate on externals and ignore what is more important, internals. They assess themselves not in regard to their hearts, nor in regard to their relationships with other people, but in regard to the law. "Have we obeyed the law?"

Jesus is constantly trying to get the Pharisees to redirect this focus and to ask themselves, "Have I acted lovingly?" By telling the Pharisees that the kingdom of God is among them Jesus seems once more to be emphasizing internal and relational considerations rather than external considerations.

154

However, this is not a statement to be taken in isolation when one is trying to understand what Jesus means when he uses the metaphor "kingdom."

"Kingdom" is, after all, a metaphor, a comparison. In using this word Jesus is trying to describe a spiritual reality which is, in some way, comparable to a kingdom on earth. In what ways is it comparable? This is a question that we will have to keep in mind because there is no single answer. When we try to understand the "kingdom" we are definitely probing a mystery. That is why so many of the parables begin, "The kingdom of God is like . . . ." Many of the parables are exploring the metaphor "kingdom."

One of these parables was told to correct the misimpression that the kingdom of God was to appear immediately. This is the parable of the pounds which we discussed in Matthew's gospel (Luke 19:11–27). As was said earlier, the parable teaches that one should not, out of fear, refuse to use one's gifts while waiting for the coming of the kingdom. This parable gives one the idea that the kingdom is a future event.

How can the kingdom be both a present relationship and a future event? Perhaps some light can be cast on this mystery by looking at two comparisons which appear in the thirteenth chapter of Luke's gospel. "What is the kingdom of God like? And to what shall I compare it? It is like a grain of mustard seed which a man took and sowed in his garden; and it grew and became a tree, and the birds of the air made nests in its branches."

And again he said, "To what shall I compare the kingdom of God? It is like leaven which a woman took and hid in three measures of flour, till it was all leavened" (Luke 13:18–21).

In each of these comparisons the kingdom is compared to a growth process. A mustard seed cannot actually be seen growing into a tree. However, the effect of the growth process can certainly be seen. In hindsight the difference between what the tree has become and what it used to be is perfectly obvious.

The same is true of the effect of yeast on a loaf of bread. The effect of the yeast on the loaf is certainly apparent even though one cannot actually see the yeast working.

When one thinks of the kingdom as a growth process the apparent contradiction between thinking of the kingdom as a present relationship and thinking of it as a future event becomes more understandable. The kingdom is evidently a reality which is partially present but which is not completely present because it involves a growth process.

Therefore, the kingdom is both "right now" and "not yet." It is "right now" in that it has become accessible through Jesus. However, it is "not yet" because the process of the coming of the kingdom is not complete. This "right now but not yet" aspect of the kingdom is only one of the paradoxes with which we must grapple when we try to understand what Jesus meant when he used the metaphor "kingdom."

Review Questions

1. What is a paradox?
2. How do the Pharisees assess themselves?
3. How does Jesus think the Pharisees should assess themselves?
4. What does Jesus mean when he tells the Pharisees that the kingdom of God is among them?
5. What do we mean when we say that "kingdom" is a metaphor?
6. How can the kingdom be both a present reality and a future event?

Discussion Questions

1. Did you examine your conscience when you were little? How? Do you examine your conscience now? How? What questions do you think Jesus would have us ask ourselves in an examination of conscience?
2. Do you think the kingdom of God is in any way already present? How?
3. In the "Our Father" when you pray, "Thy kingdom come," for what do you think you are praying?

Kingdom: A Once in a
Lifetime Chance?

Question: "Is the invitation to the kingdom a once in a lifetime opportunity or do people have many chances to say 'yes'?" (Luke 8:8; 13:8–9; 14:15–24; 20:9–16; 20:19)

Again, the "either-or" way in which this question is framed makes it difficult to answer. It seems that the invitation to the kingdom is an urgent invitation. It also seems that the invitation is not eternal. Nevertheless, the invitation seems to be offered over time. Let us look at Luke's gospel to see that all three of these statements seem to be true.

Whenever Jesus speaks about the kingdom he seems to speak with urgency. For example, when Jesus teaches about the kingdom of God through the parable of the sower he expresses real urgency about his message to be good soil. We can hear the urgency in his voice when he concludes with, "He who has ears to hear, let him hear" (Luke 8:8).

Since Jesus' message was urgent he became exasperated, even angry, with those who refused the invitation to the kingdom. Jesus warned the Pharisees that the invitation is not eternal when he told them the parable of the wicked tenants (Luke 20:9–16).

In this parable a man plants a vineyard and lets it out to tenants. In time he sends first one servant, then a second and a third to the tenants, but they abuse each servant and send each away empty-handed. Next the owner sends his own son, but the tenants kill the son. Jesus then asks, "What will the owner of the vineyard do to them? He will come and destroy those tenants and give the vineyard to others" (Luke 20:15–16).

The Pharisees compare to the wicked tenants who abuse those sent by the owner of the vineyard. They realize that Jesus has aimed this parable at them. Luke tells us they understand and therefore want to destroy Jesus. "The scribes and chief priests tried to lay hands on him at that very hour, but they feared the people; they perceived that he had told this parable against them" (Luke 20:19).

Jesus has made it clear to the Pharisees that the invitation to the kingdom will not last forever. At some point the invitation will be withdrawn.

Another parable, while much less acrimonious, also suggests that the invitation to the kingdom might be extended over time, but is not eternal. This is the parable of the fig tree (Luke 13:6–9). A man who has a fig tree in his vineyard gets fed up when the fig tree fails to yield fruit over three years. So he tells the vinedresser to cut the tree down. The vinedresser responds, "Let it alone, sir, this year also, till I dig about it and put on manure. And if it bears fruit next year, well and good; but if not, you can cut it down" (Luke 13:8–9).

Once again it seems that the invitation to be fruitful is extended over time, but that does not mean that the invitation will always be extended. At some point, if the tree remains fruitless, it will be cut down.

Still another parable which reflects this same state of affairs is one which is similar to a parable which appeared in Matthew's gospel. This is Luke's parable of the great banquet (Luke 14:15–24). Jesus is at a Pharisee's house when his host says, "Blessed is he who shall eat bread in the kingdom of God" (Luke 14:15). Jesus responds to this comment with a parable about a man who invited many guests to his banquet. However, the guests made one excuse after another and did not come. The master was very angry and sent his servant out not once, but twice, to compel people to come. "Go to the highways and hedges, and compel people to come in, that my house may be filled. For I tell you,

---

PARADOXES ABOUT THE KINGDOM

Future and Present
An Event and A Process
External and Internal
Triumph of Good and Co-existence with Evil
Earned and A Gift Wholeheartedly Accepted
Good News as Future Reward and Good News as Present Reality
Look for Final Judgment and Be Ready Now
Urgent Choice and Constant Invitation
Place Entered at Death and Relationship Entered at Baptism
For Some and For All

---

none of those men who were invited shall taste my banquet" (Luke 14:23–24).

Through this parable Jesus is telling the Pharisees that it is no great feat to be invited to the kingdom. The invitation is forced on people. The problem is that many refuse the invitation. Those who are not in the kingdom will be those who have refused to come.

In all of these parables, then, it seems that Jesus is teaching that the invitation to the kingdom is an urgent invitation, one which one may lose if one does not respond. Nevertheless, the invitation is offered over time, and no one knows when the invitation will be withdrawn.

Review Questions

1. What does the parable of the wicked tenants teach about the kingdom?
2. What does the parable of the fig tree teach about the kingdom?
3. What does the parable of the great banquet teach about the kingdom?
4. Is the invitation to the kingdom an urgent invitation? Why or why not?

Discussion Questions

1. Do you think that you have been invited to the kingdom? Why or why not?
2. Do you have a choice about being invited to the kingdom? Why or why not?
3. Do you think there is any urgency about responding to this invitation? Why or why not?

ARTICLE 12

Love for the "Lost"

Question: "I agree with the older brother in the parable of the prodigal son (Luke 15:11–32). Why does he turn out to be the bad guy in the story?" (Luke 15:3–7; 15:8–10)

Many people who read the parable of the prodigal son react as this questioner did. After all, the older brother is accurate in what he says about himself. "Lo, these many years I have served you, and I never disobeyed your command: yet you never gave me a kid, that I might make merry with my friends" (Luke 15:29). What fault can be found with the older brother?

In order to understand the lesson which Jesus is teaching his audience through this parable we must remember that a parable is the middle of a conversation. To whom is Jesus telling this story, and why?

The parable of the prodigal son is one of three parables which Luke has placed in the same social context. So we must read the passage before the first of these three parables in order to understand the conversation. Luke tells us, "Now the tax collectors and sinners were all drawing near to hear him. And the Pharisees and the scribes murmured saying, 'This man receives sinners and eats with them' " (Luke 15:1–2).

The first parable which follows this statement is the parable of the lost sheep (Luke 15:3–7). Luke has Jesus tell us the lesson of this parable. "I tell you, there will be more joy in heaven over one sinner who repents than over ninety-nine righteous persons who need no repentance" (Luke 15:7). We can, of course, hear irony in the word "righteous" since there is no one in Jesus' audience who has no need of repentance.

161

The second parable, similar to the first, is the parable of the lost coin (Luke 15:8–10). Again Luke places the lesson to be learned on Jesus' lips. "Just so, I tell you, there is joy before the angels of God over one sinner who repents" (Luke 15:10).

Next Jesus tells the parable of the prodigal son. At first this parable seems similar to the other two. However, this appearance is deceptive and part of Jesus' plan. Through the parable of the prodigal son Jesus hopes to help the Pharisees realize that they too are sinners in need of repentance. He does this by telling them a story which they originally understand to be a third parable about seeking out that which is lost. Since they don't think of themselves as lost they do not expect the story to have any personal impact on them, any call to conversion for them. So they let down their defenses and listen to the story.

As Jesus tells these self-righteous Pharisees the story of the man with two sons, the Pharisees do not identify with the younger son. They are good people, faithful people, law-abiding people. They would never act as the younger son did.

As the story continues a character is introduced with whom the Pharisees do identify. The older brother is just like the Pharisees. He has always done what his father requested. He sees himself as far superior to his sinful brother. He is completely blind to the fact that, in failing to forgive and welcome his brother, in failing to love his brother, he is himself sinning. This older brother is indeed just like the Pharisees.

The father of the two sons treats each of his sinful sons with love. For each son the father comes out. The younger son has already realized and repented of his sin when the father comes out. The older son had done neither. The older son explains his feelings to his father, just as we saw the Pharisees do before any of the three parables were told. However, he does not see his own lack of love, and so he does not repent of this sin.

When the Pharisees heard this story they would have realized only in hindsight that the story was about them. But as they mulled over the story, agreeing with the older brother, just as our questioner did, they might well realize that Jesus was reaching out to them and inviting them to a change of heart, just as the father in the story had reached out to his obedient, self-righteous older son.

Review Questions

1. To whom does Jesus tell the parable of the prodigal son? What criticism, aimed at Jesus, triggers the story?
2. What is the lesson in the parable of the lost sheep?
3. What is the lesson in the parable of the lost coin?
4. With which character in the parable of the prodigal son do the Pharisees compare? How are they alike?
5. What is Jesus teaching the Pharisees through the parable of the prodigal son?

Discussion Questions

1. Do you side with the older brother when you hear the parable of the prodigal son? Why or why not?
2. Do you believe that God always welcomes back the sinner? Do you think God should? Why or why not? Do you think you should? Why or why not?

ARTICLE 13

Humorous Irony Used To Correct

Question: "Why does Jesus praise the dishonest steward (Luke 16:1–9)? This parable doesn't make any sense at all."

In order to understand the parable of the dishonest steward we will have to put into practice the methodology we have been learning. We have in these verses a parable followed by an ironic statement. If one knows how to interpret a parable and if one is able to recognize irony, there is no problem with this text. It makes a great deal of sense.

In the parable of the dishonest steward Jesus tells the story of a steward who heard that he would soon lose his job. The steward decides to call his master's debtors and cancel half their debts so that they will treat him kindly when he is out of a job.

Of course, when one hears of the steward's plan, one expects the master to be furious with the steward and punish him in some way. However, "The master commended the dishonest steward for his shrewdness; for the sons of this world are more shrewd in dealing with their own generation than the sons of light" (Luke 16:8). Why would the master praise the steward?

Once more, in order to understand what Jesus is teaching his audience through the parable, we must identify the people to whom Jesus is speaking and see how they compare to a character in the story.

Jesus is telling this parable to the disciples. The disciples are like the dishonest steward not because they are dishonest but because the disciples too are in a temporary situation.

Notice that all of the steward's actions were motivated by the fact that he knew his present situation was temporary. There-

164

**SOME PARABLES ABOUT THE KINGDOM
IN LUKE'S GOSPEL**

8:4–8   The Parable of the Sower
13:6–9   The Parable of the Fig Tree
13:19   The Parable of the Mustard Seed
13:21   The Parable of the Yeast
14:16–24   The Parable of the Invited Guests Who Made
           Excuses
19:12–27   The Parable of the Pounds
20:9–15   The Parable of the Wicked Husbandman

---

fore, he acted in the present situation in order to prepare for the next situation. It is this foresight which the master praises.

The disciples, too, are in a temporary situation: earth. Children of the light know that earth is a temporary situation. Why is it that, knowing this, so few children of the light act on earth with an eye to what comes next? It is because of this lack of foresight that the master comments: "The sons of this world are more shrewd in dealing with their own generation than the sons of light" (Luke 16:18).

Jesus follows this parable with a statement which many people find puzzling because it seems to contradict the point Jesus was making in the parable. The statement is, "And I tell you, make friends for yourselves by means of unrighteous mammon, so that when it fails they may receive you into the eternal habitations" (Luke 16:9).

Only if one is able to invest Jesus' words with an ironic tone does this passage make sense. Friends bought with money can't welcome anyone into eternal habitations. The sense of the saying is, "If you want to be welcomed into eternal habitations, don't make friends with money because they can't welcome you into eternity."

The tone is identical to one a parent might use with a college-bound child who wanted to marry an eighteen year old. The parent might say, "Go ahead and get married and let your

spouse put you through college." The intent behind the statement is, "If you want to go to college don't get married because
your spouse won't be able to put you through." This kind of
irony is a humorous and gentle way to correct someone.

In the course of our study of the gospels we have seen Jesus
slip into the use of irony so often that it is fair to say that the use
of irony appears to be an integral part of Jesus' personality as he
appears in the synoptic gospels.

Review Questions

1. To whom does Jesus tell the parable of the dishonest steward?
2. With which character in the parable does the audience
   compare?
3. What is Jesus teaching his audience through the parable?
4. What is the meaning of the ironic statement which follows
   the parable?

Discussion Questions

1. Do you think many "children of the light" live with an eye to
   their next situation? Why or why not? What would living this
   way involve?
2. If one uses money to win friends do you think he or she can
   expect to be welcomed into eternity? Why or why not?
3. Do you agree that the statement after the parable is
   ironic? Why?
4. Do you think it is accurate to say that Jesus is pictured in the
   synoptic gospels as using irony often? What difference does
   this make?

ARTICLE 14

Parables: The Message
Depends on the Audience

Question: "Why doesn't God let Lazarus warn the rich man's brothers before it is too late?" (Luke 16:19–31)

The person who asked this question has fallen back into the trap of treating a parable as an allegory. God is not a character in the parable of the rich man and Lazarus. Father Abraham is, but he does not represent God.

In this parable Jesus tells the story of a rich man who ignores Lazarus, a poor man at his gate. Both the rich man and Lazarus die. Lazarus goes to Abraham's bosom and the rich man to torment in Hades.

Once in Hades the rich man asks that Lazarus comfort him, but Abraham says that no one can cross in either direction between Abraham's bosom and Hades. It is at this point that the rich man asks that someone be sent to warn his brothers. "But Abraham said, 'They have Moses and the prophets; let them hear them.' And he said, 'No, father Abraham, but if someone goes to them from the dead they will repent.' He said to him, 'If they do not hear Moses and the prophets, neither will they be convinced if someone should rise from the dead'" (Luke 16:29–31).

Many people, on reading this parable, presume that the parable is a warning against an abuse of riches. Actually, the criticism contained in the parable is not about the proper use of riches at all.

Jesus had earlier been teaching the Pharisees about the proper use of money. He had said, "No servant can serve two masters;

167

for either he will hate the one and love the other, or he will be devoted to the one and despise the other. You cannot serve God and mammon" (Luke 16:13).

Luke then tells us, "The Pharisees, who were lovers of money, heard all of this and they scoffed at him" (Luke 16:14).

It is after the Pharisees have rejected Jesus and his teaching that he tells them the story of the rich man and Lazarus.

While this parable appears to be about the proper use of riches, it soon moves on to a different theme. As with the parable of the prodigal son, Jesus lowers the defenses of his audience by beginning the story in such a way that they do not feel threatened or criticized by it. However, the story does not end with the rich man in Hades and Lazarus in the bosom of Abraham. Jesus has something else to say, and his theme moves away from the proper use of money.

The Pharisees compare to the rich man's brothers, but not because both are rich. The Pharisees are like the rich man's brothers because, as Abraham says, they have Moses and the prophets to teach them. However, like the brothers, the Pharisees are not really listening to Moses and the prophets.

Then, in a statement which Luke's audience would understand as dripping with dramatic irony, Abraham adds, "If they do not hear Moses and the prophets, neither will they be convinced if someone should rise from the dead" (Luke 16:31).

In the context of the conversation between Jesus and the Pharisees, Jesus tells the parable of the rich man and Lazarus to warn the Pharisees that as they reject Jesus and his teaching they are rejecting Moses and the prophets, since Jesus is the fulfillment of the prophets. The Pharisees, of course, do not realize that this is true. They think they are being faithful to Moses and the prophets even as they continue to scoff at Jesus.

In the context of the conversation between Luke and his audience, this final comment of Abraham's is filled with dramatic irony because Luke's audience knows that the words which Jesus aimed at the Pharisees have turned out to be exactly accurate. Not only have the Pharisees ignored Moses and the prophets but they have failed to believe even now that someone has risen from the dead.

Review Questions

1. To whom does Jesus tell the parable of the rich man and Lazarus?
2. What behavior on the audience's part triggered the story?
3. With what character in the parable does the audience compare?
4. What is Jesus teaching his audience through the parable?
5. What added meaning can be understood in Abraham's words by the time Luke is collating his gospel?

Discussion Questions

1. What do you think Jesus teaches about the proper use of riches? Why do you think the Pharisees scoffed at this teaching?
2. In what way were the Pharisees refusing to listen to Moses and the prophets?
3. What is ironic about the statement, "And they would not listen even if someone rose from the dead?" Could this statement describe us? How?

ARTICLE 15

Parables Must Be Interpreted
as Parables

Question: "Why does Jesus compare God to an unjust judge (Luke 18:1–7)? This doesn't make sense." (Luke 11:5–8; 14:7–10 also discussed)

Jesus does not compare God to an unjust judge. The mistake in the mind of the person who asked the question is once again a mistake about literary form. The questioner is interpreting a parable as though it were an allegory.

Remember, an allegory is a story with two levels of meaning. Everything on the literal level, the story line level, stands for something on the intentional level. Were this story an allegory the widow would stand for a person praying and the unjust judge would stand for God.

However, the story is not an allegory; it is a parable. Luke even introduces the story by saying it is a parable. "And he told them a parable to the effect that . . ." (Luke 18:1). So to interpret the parable we need to use our usual method of parable interpretation and find the lesson by comparing the audience to a character in the story.

This parable is directed to the disciples. They compare to the widow who did not easily give up, but kept asking for what she needed. The lesson for the disciples is to keep asking as that widow did. Luke tells us that this is the lesson before we hear the story, "They ought to always pray and not lose heart" (Luke 18:1).

The lesson, then, is identical to the one taught earlier when the disciples ask Jesus, "Teach us to pray" (Luke 11:1). In response,

Jesus asks which of them, "who has a friend, will go to him at midnight and say to him, 'Friend, lend me three loaves, for a friend of mine has arrived on a journey, and I have nothing to set before him' " (Luke 11:5-6). Even if the friend won't help because he is a friend, he will help if the person keeps asking. Again, the lesson is, "Ask, and it will be given" (Luke 11:9). However, God is not like the friend who didn't want to be bothered. We must resist our temptation to allegorize.

The parable of the widow and the unjust judge is not the only parable which Luke introduces by saying, "He told them a parable." On several occasions this is a helpful preamble because if Luke did not tell us that what follows is a parable we might misinterpret the story entirely. A case in point is the parable about taking seats at table (Luke 14:7-10). At first glance this seems to be straightforward advice about etiquette. "When you are invited by anyone to a marriage feast, do not sit down in a place of honor, lest a more eminent man than you be invited by him and he who invited you both will come and say to you, 'Give place to this man,' and then you will begin with shame to take the lowest place. But when you are invited, go and sit in the lowest place, so that when your host comes he may say to you, 'Friend, go up higher.' Then you will be honored in the presence of all who sit at table with you" (Luke 14:9-10).

However, Luke warns us that we might miss something in this apparently straightforward advice by introducing the remarks with, "Now he told a parable to those who were invited, when he marked how they chose the places of honor" (Luke 14:7). How can this be a parable?

The audience compares not only to the guests who take the places of honor in the first place but to the guests who take back seats, hoping to be moved up. In either case, their motivation is their hope that they will be honored. Jesus is gently poking fun at his audience and humorously correcting them for their self-centered behavior. To seek worldly honor is not part of the attitude of service which Jesus teaches his followers.

As with the parable of the unjust judge, Luke warns his audience that they are about to read a parable. Knowing this, the audience will be less likely to misinterpret or overlook the truth which is being taught through the parable.

Review Questions

1. Does Jesus compare God to an unjust judge? Explain.
2. What is Jesus teaching through the parable of the widow and the judge?
3. What is Jesus teaching through the parable about taking seats at table?

Discussion Questions

1. Do you think persistence in prayer is important? Why or why not?
2. Is the person who takes a back seat, hoping to be moved up, acting like a true disciple? Why or why not?

Jesus Uses Purposeful Ambiguity

Question: "What does Jesus mean when he says, 'Render to Caesar the things that are Caesar's, and to God the things that are God's' (Luke 20:25)? Is Jesus saying that the Jews should pay their taxes or not?" (Luke 20:19–20; 20:24; 20:26 also discussed.)

When Jesus says, "Render to Caesar the things that are Caesar's and to God the things that are God's," he is being purposefully ambiguous. His words could be taken to mean, "Do pay taxes," and they could be taken to mean, "Don't pay taxes." By speaking with purposeful ambiguity Jesus has skillfully avoided the trap which his questioners had set for him. Let us look at these words in their social context so that we can understand just what a brilliant answer Jesus has given.

The purpose of the question "Should we pay taxes or not?" was to trap Jesus. Luke tells us this: "The scribes and chief priests tried to lay hands on him at that very hour, but they feared the people; for they perceived that he had told this parable (i.e. the parable of the wicked tenants) against them. So they watched him and sent spies, who pretended to be sincere, so that they might take hold of what he said, so as to deliver him up to the authority and jurisdiction of the governor" (Luke 20:19–20).

No matter how Jesus answered the question he would antagonize some of his audience. The Jews, of course, resented paying taxes to the Romans. If Jesus were to say "Pay taxes," he would antagonize his own people. However, if Jesus were to say "Don't pay taxes," he would be inciting people to disobey Roman law. This would give the scribes and chief priests a reason to turn Jesus over to the Roman authorities.

In addition to the problem of paying taxes to the Romans, the Jews had an additional problem with the fact that Roman coins had Caesar's picture embossed on them. The coins were graven images in the eyes of the Jews, and to have graven images was against Jewish law.

Instead of giving a direct answer to the scribes' question Jesus asks an ironic question: "Show me a coin. Whose likeness and inscription has it?" (Luke 20:24).

This question is one more example of Jesus' use of Socratic irony. The question seems a little dim-witted. Everyone knows whose picture is on the coin.

However, if the scribes and chief priests were as faithful to their own beliefs as they want to appear to be, they would not have had these graven images with them. Since they don't say they can't show Jesus a coin we can only assume that they do produce a coin as they answer, "Caesar's" (Luke 20:24). In possessing coins they compromise themselves in the eyes of their fellow Jews.

Jesus then says, "Render to Caesar the things that are Caesar's and to God the things that are God's" (Luke 20:25). If one is Jewish and against paying taxes, one might interpret Jesus' words as meaning, "We don't deal in graven images. Those must be Caesar's." On the other hand, if one is Roman and thinks taxes should be paid, one might interpret Jesus' words as meaning, "Yes, you should pay taxes."

In addition to slipping out of the trap, Jesus admonishes these scribes and chief priests when he adds, "And render to God the things that are God's" (Luke 20:24). The scribes and chief priests are failing to render to God what they should—a loving heart.

Luke tells us that the scribes and chief priests realize they have been outsmarted. "And they were not able in the presence of the people to catch him by what he said; but marveling at his answer they were silent" (Luke 20:26).

Through his Socratic irony and his purposeful ambiguity Jesus has completely escaped the trap laid for him by his enemies.

Review Questions

1. Why would Jesus speak with "purposeful ambiguity"?
2. Why is the question about taxes dangerous to answer?
3. How did Jesus trick those who wanted to trap him when he said, "Show me a coin"?
4. What might a Jew take Jesus' answer to mean?
5. What might a Roman take Jesus' answer to mean?

Discussion Questions

1. How do you think, "Render to Caesar the things that are Caesar's and to God the things that are God's," corrected the Pharisees?
2. In the context of our lives what might Jesus' words be interpreted to mean? Do you think they could fairly be interpreted to mean, "Be a good citizen. Vote." Why or why not?

ARTICLE 17

Jesus' Words on the Cross

Question: "Why is it that Jesus' words on the cross are different in Luke's gospel than they were in Mark's and Matthew's" (Luke 23:39–46)? (Luke 22:41; 22:43; 22:51; 22:61; 23:34; Mark 14:15; 14:35; 14:52; 15:34; Matthew 27:46; Psalm 22 also discussed)

Since in the passion narrative we are dealing with literature which has come through oral tradition we know that any expectation on our part that we are reading exact quotations is misplaced. However, the questioner may not be asking for a "literary form" explanation of why the words are not identical. Rather, he may be probing more deeply and asking about the pastoral reasons for the differences.

Since Mark's and Matthew's passion narratives are quite similar we will compare only Mark's and Luke's in this article. What is Mark emphasizing for his audience of persecuted Christians? What is Luke emphasizing for his audience of Gentiles? How do Jesus' words on the cross in each gospel fit into this emphasis?

In Mark's gospel Jesus' last words are, "My God, my God, why hast thou forsaken me?" (Mark 15:34). These words accurately sum up the emphasis throughout Mark's passion narrative. In reading Mark's gospel one gets a picture of Jesus as being totally abandoned. We have already noted that the apostles fail him, falling asleep three times when he has asked them to pray. As Jesus is arrested, "all forsook him and fled" (Mark 14:50). One young man, who had been wearing nothing but a linen cloth, was seized. In order to escape he left the cloth and ran

176

away naked (Mark 14:52). What a graphic illustration of the opposite of discipleship! A disciple would have left all to follow Jesus.

At no time during Jesus' passion, as it is pictured in Mark's gospel, does Jesus receive any comfort. No angel ministers to him as is true in Luke (Luke 22:43). No one grieves over him as some do in Luke (Luke 22:27). No thief on the cross defends Jesus as one does in Luke (Luke 23:39–42).

The words "My God, my God, why hast thou forsaken me?" (Mark 15:34) continue this theme of Jesus' experience of abandonment.

However, these words do not reflect despair on Jesus' part. Rather they show Jesus saying a prayer that would have been familiar to Mark's audience—Psalm 22. The prayer starts with the psalmist's present feeling of abandonment, but it moves on to the psalmist's experience of faith and trust that Yahweh will save as he has in the past.

Since Mark's audience may, like Jesus, be going to have to face death in order to be faithful to their vocations, Mark emphasizes the fact that embracing death was not easy for Jesus either. Mark's abandoned Jesus is one with whom Mark's audience would be able to identify and thus be able to follow through death to resurrection.

In Luke's gospel Jesus speaks from the cross three times. First he speaks words of forgiveness: "Father, forgive them, for they know not what they do" (Luke 23:34). Next he promises his kingdom to the penitent thief: "Truly, I say to you, today you will be with me in paradise" (Luke 23:43). And finally he speaks words of love and trust: "Father, into thy hands I commit my spirit" (Luke 23:46).

Once again the words on the cross reflect the tone of the whole passion narrative, and indeed of Luke's whole gospel. In Luke's gospel Jesus is not so distressed over his own situation that he fails to minister to others. Even as he is arrested Jesus heals the ear of the soldier who has come to arrest him (Luke 22:51). And when Peter denies Jesus, only Luke tells us, "The Lord turned and looked at Peter" (Luke 22:61). What did Peter see in Jesus'

JESUS' WORDS ON THE CROSS

In Mark's Gospel
   15:34   "Eloi, Eloi, lama sabachthani? My God, my God, why have you deserted me?"

In Matthew's Gospel
   27:46   "Eli, Eli, Lama sabachthani. My God, my God, why have you deserted me?"

In Luke's Gospel
   23:34   "Father, forgive them; they do not know what they are doing."
   23:43   "Indeed, I promise you, today you will be with me in paradise."
   23:46   "Father, into thy hands I commit my Spirit."

In John's Gospel
   19:26–27 "Woman, this is your son. This is your mother."
   19:28   "I am thirsty."
   19:30   "It is accomplished."

---

eyes? Luke does not specifically tell us, but from the gospel as a whole we know that Peter saw love. No wonder Peter wept.

Nowhere in Luke's gospel is Jesus as distressed as he appeared in Mark. At the beginning of his passion he does not fall on the ground to pray as he did in Mark (Mark 14:35). Rather, he kneels (Luke 22:41). And at the end of his passion he expresses no feeling of abandonment, but rather one of closeness to his Father. "Father, into thy hands I commit my spirit" (Luke 23:46).

This trusting, non-judgmental, and forgiving attitude is present not only in Luke's passion narrative but, as we have seen, throughout his gospel. Luke wants his Gentile audience to understand the all-embracing love of Jesus, love which will embrace even Gentiles in the covenant relationship.

The words on the cross do differ in each gospel, and in each gospel they reflect the pastoral concerns of the gospel editor.

Review Questions

1. What are Jesus' words on the cross in each gospel?
2. What picture of Jesus predominates in Mark's account? Why is this emphasis appropriate for Mark's audience?
3. What picture of Jesus is predominant in Luke's account? Why is this emphasis appropriate for Luke's audience?

Discussion Questions

1. Do you find it upsetting to realize that the accounts differ in regard to Jesus' words on the cross? Why or why not?
2. Do you prefer Mark's picture of Jesus during the passion, or Luke's? Why?
3. What do you think it means to act pastorally? Do you think Mark and Luke have acted pastorally in their accounts? Why or why not?

ARTICLE 18

Appearance Stories:
Accounts of Faith Experiences

Question: "Why did Jesus' followers not recognize him when he appeared to them on the road to Emmaus?" (Luke 24:13–35; Luke 24:36–47 also discussed)

The story of the disciples on the road to Emmaus, like other appearance stories, pictures people who knew Jesus well as unable to recognize him after the resurrection. Why? In order to answer this question we should first ask ourselves, "What kind of writing is an 'appearance story'?"

The appearance stories grew up in the early faith community separate from the gospel as a whole, as did infancy narratives, miracle stories, collections of sayings, etc. The function of the appearance stories was not, as a twentieth century reader often presumes, to give a literal account of an historical event. Rather, the function was to give a helpful account of a faith experience.

So the questions now become: "What is the faith experience that is being expressed through the story?" and "How is the story helpful to the audience?"

To say that the account is about a faith experience rather than an event is not to say that no event occurred. What is the difference between an event and a faith experience? Both are real, but an event can happen despite the receptivity of the person. A faith experience has a subjective dimension.

The involvement of the person is an integral component of a faith experience. Something is happening outside the person, but something is happening inside the person, too.

All of our accounts of Jesus' post-resurrection appearances are about appearances to those who became his followers. It seems that just as one needed faith in order to experience the historical Jesus' healing power ("He could work no miracles there"—see Mark 6:5–6), so one needed faith in order to experience the presence of the risen Christ.

The faith experience of the members of the early church was that Jesus was alive after he had died. They experienced his presence as "bodily," but it was a very different kind of body. How might this experience of "a body, but a very different kind of body" be made clear to an audience?

Precise language is impossible here. We do not have words for brand new experiences. However, this experience could be dramatized in several ways.

One is by showing Jesus in the company of people who know him well but don't recognize him, as occurs with the disciples on the road to Emmaus (Luke 24:13–35).

Others are to have Jesus suddenly appear in a room and show him inviting people to touch him or asking for something to eat (Luke 24:36–47). These dramatic details all function to assert the "bodily" presence of the resurrected Lord while warning that the "body" in question is not what one might expect.

What is a resurrected body like? We don't know, but we shouldn't assume that "body" is synonymous with "flesh." If these words were synonymous, Paul's phrase "spiritual body" would not make sense, nor would his statement that flesh and blood do not inherit eternal life.

Rather than thinking just in terms of flesh we might think of the body as that which individualizes us and as that which allows us to be in communication with others. These ideas of body existed in the Greek and Hebrew cultures in which the appearance stories originated.

Although the disciples on the road to Emmaus did not originally recognize Jesus, they did recognize him "in the breaking of the bread" (Luke 24:35). This is the way Luke's audience, and we ourselves, must learn to recognize the presence of the risen Lord. Luke's audience, and we, may, like the disciples on the road, have trouble recognizing the body of Christ. But as we listen to the word and break bread together, as the disciples did, our eyes too will be opened and we will grow in our ability to recognize the body of Christ.

Review Questions

1. What is the function of an appearance story?
2. What is the difference between an event and a faith experience?
3. How might one dramatize one's experience of the resurrected Jesus as having a body but a very different kind of body?
4. What ideas of "body" existed in Greek and Hebrew culture?
5. How did the disciples on the road finally recognize Jesus? What is the significance of this?

Discussion Questions

1. Do you understand what is meant by a "faith experience"? Do you have any personal experience which helps you understand? Explain.
2. Do you equate "body" and "flesh"? What other ideas of "body" are there? How do you imagine a resurrected body?
3. What do you think Luke is telling his audience when he says that the disciples recognized Jesus in the word and in the breaking of the bread?
4. Do you recognize Christ's body? Where? When?

Summation and Transition
from Luke's to John's Gospel

You have now read the "synoptic gospels," that is, the gospels of Mark, Matthew and Luke. These gospels are accurately called "synoptic" because, despite the fact that each is unique in its arrangement and emphasis, these gospels can be "seen as one."

In terms of methodology, what we learned about Mark we could also apply to Matthew and Luke. Jesus' relationship with other groups—the crowds, the Pharisees and the disciples—were basically the same in each gospel. Jesus' preaching about the kingdom was the same. Jesus' method of teaching through parables was the same. Anyone who read any of these gospels would immediately recognize their similarities.

As you move from the synoptic gospels to the gospel according to John you will not have this sense of being on familiar ground. While your knowledge of the synoptics will be essential for your understanding of John, you will not be able to understand John simply by applying what you have learned about the synoptics. Reading John will be like visiting a familiar friend, Jesus, in a different country where his language and manner have changed.

So, try to take as little baggage as possible with you, and read John's gospel as you would a novel. Try to enter John's world and let his gospel, too, speak for itself. Don't stop to read footnotes, introductions, or commentaries. Just read the gospel from beginning to end, jotting down your questions as you go. Only if you read the gospel first will you get a sense of it as a whole. Many of the questions which you have will be addressed in the following articles.

THE GOSPEL ACCORDING
to John

ARTICLE 1

John's Method and Message

Question: "I don't really understand the beginning of John's gospel, but it reminds me of the story of creation in Genesis when it starts, 'In the beginning,' and talks about creation. Is the main idea here that God created the world?"

The prologue to John's gospel (John 1:1–18) is designed to echo the first words of the creation story in Genesis, but the main idea of the prologue is not that God created the world. Rather, the prologue is centering in on the question, "Who is Jesus Christ?"

However, the subject of creation does play a role in answering this question for two reasons: one has to do with John's method, the second with his message.

In regard to John's method, all through John's gospel the created, material world and the event level of the narrative are used to talk about another realm of reality entirely, the spiritual realm. John's gospel is about creation, but not creation of earth, sun, moon, and stars. Rather, it is about a new creation, the new spiritual order which exists as a result of Jesus Christ.

When one level of a narrative, the literal level, is used to discuss another topic entirely, the intentional level, the author is using a kind of writing called allegory. We will have constant opportunity to give examples of John's allegorical method and to explore his allegorical message as we read the rest of John's gospel.

187

WHEN DID JESUS BECOME DIVINE?

- Mark's gospel—At least from his baptism on.
- Matthew's gospel—At least from his conception on.
- Luke's gospel—The "firstborn" was divine even before his conception.
- John's gospel—Always. In the beginning the Word was with God. The Word became flesh and dwelt among us.

The gospels do not contradict each other on this point. They reflect the process of a growing christology in which an understanding of when Jesus became divine is pushed back in time from the resurrection to before time.

In regard to John's message, creation plays a role because John understands Jesus to be the Word through whom all that has been created came to be.

> All things were made through him, and without him was not anything made that was made (John 1:3).

In other words, John begins his gospel by placing Jesus in a much wider context than did the synoptic gospels. As we know, knowledge of who Jesus actually was developed only after the resurrection. As Jesus' followers began to understand that he was divine, the question might have been asked, "When did Jesus become divine?" As we saw when reading the synoptics, a perception of Jesus' divinity is pushed backward in each succeeding gospel. Jesus' divinity is apparent in Mark only at his baptism, and in Matthew at Jesus' conception. In Luke we suggested that the word "firstborn" alluded to Jesus' cosmic role as the first-born of all creation. In John's gospel this cosmic role of Jesus' is the context for the whole gospel. Jesus is seen as the preexistent Word who, although not identical with, is one with the Father.

The Word was with God, and the Word was God (John 1:2).

Jesus' relationship to the Father is what makes it possible for Jesus to be the "Word" or the complete revelation of God.

Many scholars suggest that the prologue to John's gospel was a hymn which had grown up in liturgical settings and which was appropriated by John and adapted to introduce his gospel. Through this prologue John introduces the major themes which we will see recur over and over throughout the gospel. Among these themes are: that a new spiritual order exists in and through Christ; that Jesus is one with the Father and perfectly reveals the Father; that all life comes from Jesus; that Jesus, as the one who reveals the Father, is light to the world, a light which cannot be overcome by darkness; that this creating and revealing Word took on flesh and lived on earth; and that all grace and truth come not through Moses and the law, but through Jesus Christ.

We will also have constant opportunity to explore these themes which are central to John's gospel. They occur and reoccur so often that one sometimes feels that the gospel lacks organization, that it fails to move forward. Actually the gospel is carefully organized. These themes could be compared to strands in a rope which, once introduced in the opening prologue, are braided together throughout the gospel. Through both dialogues and monologues John will delve deeper and deeper into the mysteries which he has introduced.

As we read John's gospel, then, we will see that through an allegorical "event" level and through dialogues which explore major themes, the author of John's gospel shares with his readers his deep spiritual insights about Jesus Christ, the Word who became flesh and dwells among us.

Review Questions

1. What question does the prologue of John's gospel address?
2. What is John's method?
3. Who does John understand Jesus to be?

4. What is Jesus' relationship to the Father?
5. Name six themes which John introduces in his prologue.

Discussion Questions

1. What do the words "and the Word became flesh" mean to you? Does the fact that "the Word became flesh" affect your life in any way? Explain.
2. What do you think it means to say, "Jesus is light to the world"?
3. John says, "He came to his own and his own received him not." Do you think there is any truth to these words today? Explain.

ARTICLE 2

John: Author or Editor?

Question: "When you say that John appropriated and revised a hymn to introduce his gospel are you saying that John is the author of the gospel in the real sense of the word "author" or is this gospel an edited arrangement of inherited sources as were the synoptic gospels?"

John's gospel is not the same kind of writing as were Mark's, Matthew's and Luke's gospels, but neither is it entirely the work of one person.

It is obvious that John's gospel has an entirely different flavor than do the synoptics. In the synoptics we saw Jesus preach the kingdom of God, often through parables. We saw Jesus perform many miracles, among them exorcisms. We heard Jesus preach about the end of the world and about the "Son of Man" coming on the clouds of heaven. As you will see, none of these statements can be made about John's gospel.

In John you will read about only seven great "signs," some of which do not appear in the synoptic gospels at all. Interwoven with these signs you will find long theological discourses which explain the allegorical significance of the signs. In these discourses Jesus uses a completely different vocabulary than he did in the synoptics. Instead of parables you will read statements such as, "I am the light of the world," "I am the bread of life," "I am the way, the truth and the light." Jesus has a very different manner of teaching in John's gospel.

In addition to presenting a different mode of teaching, John presents a different time scheme than did the synoptics. In John's gospel you will notice that three passovers occur, so Jesus'

191

ministry is spread over a three year period instead of the single year pictured in the synoptics. The timing of Jesus' death is different in John too. Instead of dying the day after the passover meal as he does in the synoptics, John's Jesus dies at the same time the passover lamb is slain in preparation for the passover meal.

Why do all of these differences occur? We will suggest reasons for John's approach as we read these specific passages in the gospel. For now let us say that the unique vocabulary, timing and tone of John's gospel lead scripture scholars to believe that the gospel is largely the composition of one inspired author.

However, it is not completely the composition of one inspired author. The text itself shows some lack of continuity which suggests that the manuscript did not take its present form at one time. It seems that speeches were inserted in an existing text that, to some extent, disrupted the existing text. For instance, chapter 14 ends with, "Rise, let us go hence" (John 14:31). Next Jesus gives a long discourse which lasts for three chapters. Chapter 18 then begins, "When Jesus had spoken these words he went forth with his disciples across the Kidron Valley" (John 18:1). The three chapter discourse seems to have been inserted.

At the very least, the gospel seems to have been composed in stages. The original inspired author could have written it in stages himself or, after his death, the author's disciples could have inserted discourses which the author had composed at a later date.

The original author seems to have ended his gospel at chapter 20 with the closing remark, "Now Jesus did many other signs in the presence of the disciples which are not written in this book, but these are written that you may believe that Jesus is the Christ, the Son of God, and that believing you may have life in his name" (John 20:30). The final chapter, scholars believe, was added by the disciples of the author.

Was this author, referred to in the added chapter as the beloved disciple, John, the son of Zebedee? The late date of this gospel, probably around 90 A.D., makes such a conclusion unlikely. However, the author was certainly a beloved disciple and

MARK'S, MATTHEW'S, LUKE'S AND JOHN'S GOSPELS

	Mark	Matthew	Luke	John
Date	65 A.D.	80 A.D.	85 A.D.	90–95 A.D.
Audience	Persecuted Christians	Settled Jewish Christians	Gentiles	Christians who have lived past the expected time of the "second coming"
Sources	The inherited oral and written traditions of the believing community	Mark "Q" "M"	Mark "Q" "L"	The *content* of the synoptic tradition
Organization	The passion, death and resurrection preceded by some miracle stories and some controversies with the Pharisees	An infancy narrative; five thematic sections each containing a narrative and a speech by Jesus; an account of the passion, death, and resurrection	An infancy narrative; a geographic organization: Jesus has a Galilean ministry; a trip to Jerusalem, and a Jerusalem ministry; an account of the passion, death, and resurrection	A prologue; "The Book of Signs": The seven "signs" interwound with dialogue/monologues which explain the significance of the signs; An account of the passion, death, and resurrection
Theme	"Why would anyone suffer?" Look to Christ and see that suffering leads to resurrection	Jesus is the new Moses with authority from God to give the new law	The covenant relationship is universal	The "Word" became flesh and dwelt among us; look for Christ in the church and in the sacraments
Goes back to	The baptism of Jesus	A genealogy to Abraham	A genealogy to Adam	Before creation

blessed with the spiritual insight of a mystic. As we enter the world of this inspired author, knowing what we now know about the gospel's composition, we will understand the reason for an occasional lack of continuity and so will not be distracted by this. We will be able to open ourselves to the beauty of John's gospel and see why his gospel adds new depth to our understanding of the good news which we have already read in the synoptic gospels.

Review Questions

1. Name four differences between the synoptic gospels and John's gospel.
2. What function do the long theological discourses have in John's gospel?
3. Name two ways in which the timing of Jesus' ministry is different in John's gospel than it was in the synoptics.
4. What conclusion do scripture scholars draw from the unique vocabulary, timing, and tone of John's gospel?
5. Why do scripture scholars think that the gospel as we have it was not written at one time? Give two possible solutions to this problem.
6. When was this gospel written?

Discussion Questions

1. Does the fact that John's gospel is different from the synoptics in vocabulary and organization challenge your belief that all four gospels are revelation? Why or why not?
2. Does what you have learned about the composition of John's gospel challenge your belief that the gospel is inspired? Why or why not?

ARTICLE 3

Jesus: The Lamb of God

Question: "Both John the Baptist (John 1:29) and the apostles (John 1:35–51) seem to recognize who Jesus is immediately. I thought the apostles, at least, didn't realize who Jesus was until after the resurrection. What gives?"

This question hits to the core of the question of literary form. The questioner is thinking of the event level. Did Jesus' contemporaries understand who Jesus was before the resurrection? The picture we get in the synoptic gospels is clear. The apostles were not able to comprehend the truth of Jesus' identity until after the resurrection. However, the questioner is right in saying that in John's gospel both John the Baptist and the apostles seem to comprehend more about Jesus' identity from the beginning of Jesus' ministry.

John the Baptist's first words on seeing Jesus in this gospel are, "Behold the Lamb of God, who takes away the sins of the world! This is he of whom I said, 'After me comes a man who ranks before me, for he was before me' " (John 1:29–30).

John the Baptist repeats this witness to two of his disciples the very next day. On seeing Jesus he says to the disciples, "Behold the Lamb of God" (John 1:36). On hearing this, the disciples immediately follow Jesus.

What are we to make of this? Are the gospels disagreeing? Is one right and one wrong?

In order to answer these questions we must focus in on the literary form of John's gospel. What kind of writing is this? What is John intending to accomplish through his gospel? What does

195

John want his audience, probably in Ephesus, to learn as they read his gospel?

As long as we address questions that deal with the historical level to John's gospel we will completely miss John's point. That is not to say that John's gospel has no relationship to history. After all, John is writing about an historical person who lived, taught, healed, and was crucified earlier in the same century in which John is writing. John presumes that his end of the century audience knows what happened on the historical level. John is interested in teaching his audience something on the theological level. He wants to move away from the historical level, the level of events and the material word, to another level of reality entirely. He wants to delve into deep spiritual mysteries.

The passage we just quoted, where John the Baptist immediately gives witness to Jesus as the "Lamb of God," is a perfect example of John's purpose and method.

Notice that John presumes that his audience knows the historical level. When John introduces the witness of John the Baptist he gives not a word of introduction about who John the Baptist is. The reason you know the identity of John the Baptist is that you have read the synoptic gospels. You bring your knowledge of the content of the synoptics to John, and this knowledge of the basic story is a necessary background for understanding John's gospel. Obviously the author of John's gospel is presuming that his audience knows what you know from having read the synoptics. John's audience and you must bring that knowledge with you, but John intends to teach "something in addition to" that basic story, not "something instead of" nor "more of the same."

What is the author teaching by having the very first witness to Jesus be, "Behold the Lamb of God"? What does the phrase "Lamb of God" mean?

By saying that Jesus is the Lamb of God the author is making two comparisons. First the author is comparing Jesus to the paschal lamb of the Passover celebration. Second, the author is comparing Jesus to the lamb in Isaiah who was led to the slaughterhouse, never opening his mouth, the lamb who accomplished God's will of atonement for his people (see Isaiah 52:13–53:12).

Before we explore each of these comparisons let us first note that by introducing Jesus as the Lamb of God, the author of John's gospel has John the Baptist give witness to the deep theological insights which the author is teaching his end of the century audience. To ask questions at the level of history is to completely miss the point.

The theological truths taught through the phrase "Lamb of God" get to the core of John's gospel. Who is this Jesus?

Through the comparison with the paschal lamb John is presenting Jesus as the lamb whose blood gives life to his people. The passover celebration was a celebration of the passage from slavery in Egypt to freedom in the holy land.

You are probably familiar with the stories about the difficulty Moses had in getting his people out of Egypt, and the plagues which occurred. The Israelites were spared from the last plague, the death of the children, because the blood of a lamb had been placed on the lintels. The angel of death had passed over the homes of the Israelites, and their children had lived. A lamb was slaughtered as part of the yearly passover celebration in order to recall and celebrate God's saving power.

In calling Jesus the Lamb of God, then, John is comparing Jesus to this paschal lamb. However, Jesus, as the Lamb of God, saved his people not just from slavery on earth and physical death but from slavery to sin and eternal death.

As you will see, John continues this comparison of Jesus to the passover lamb in his passion narrative by having Jesus die at the same time that the paschal lambs were slaughtered before the passover celebration. That is why John moves up the passion and death twenty-four hours as compared to the synoptics. In John, Jesus is already dead before the passover because he is the paschal lamb.

John's phrase "Lamb of God" also compares Jesus to the lamb in Isaiah, the suffering servant whose suffering saved all. That Jesus would be a suffering servant rather than a glorious king is core to Jesus' identity. It is the "suffering servant" aspect of Jesus as the messiah that was completely incomprehensible to his contemporaries. The messiah as suffering servant is definitely a post-resurrection understanding.

In order to understand John's gospel, then, we must remember that John is assuming that our questions are not about history. We must ask John theological questions in order to hear what John has to say.

Review Questions

1. Historically, did the apostles understand Jesus' identity immediately or only after the resurrection? What evidence do you have to support your opinion?
2. What two comparisons is John making by calling Jesus "the Lamb of God"? Explain each.
3. What kind of questions do we need to ask of John's gospel in order to understand what the author is trying to teach?

Discussion Questions

1. Is the phrase "Lamb of God" familiar to you? Why?
2. What does it mean to say that the author of John presumes your knowledge of the content of the synoptic gospels?
3. How can we say that John's gospel teaches "something in addition to the synoptics" rather than "something instead of the synoptics" when we have just seen that in the synoptics Jesus' identity is recognized only after the resurrection and that in John's gospel John the Baptist recognizes Jesus' identity immediately? Is this a contradiction or not?

ARTICLE 4

The Wedding Feast at Cana

Question "At the wedding feast at Cana, why does Jesus call Mary 'woman,' and rebuff her (John 2:4)? This seems rude."

The story of the wedding feast at Cana is the occasion for the first of the mighty signs which Jesus works in John's gospel. In order to understand what John is teaching his audience we need to remember John's method. John uses the event level of his narrative as an allegory to teach something about the spiritual world.

Notice that the person who asked this question brought to John's gospel her knowledge of the basic facts of Jesus' life. Otherwise she would not have called Jesus' mother "Mary." Jesus' mother's name is never mentioned in John's gospel. It is not a disadvantage that we bring our knowledge of Jesus' story to John's gospel. John is depending on his audience's ability to do that. John is not trying to retell that story but to use that story, which we already know, to teach something else.

Jesus' words to Mary after his comment about the wine are, "O woman, what have you to do with me? My hour has not yet come" (John 2:4). These words do sound rude and abrupt if one understands them only on the literal level. The very fact that this is true, that the literal level seems inconsistent with the knowledge which we bring to the text, invites us to look beyond the literal level and explore this whole scene as an allegory.

The account begins, "On the third day there was a marriage at Cana" (John 2:1). If we were to add up the days to which John has referred (see John 1:29; 1:35; 1:43), we would see that the marriage feast at Cana is on the seventh day. In the book of

199

Genesis, when material creation is described, God finishes his work in six days and so rests on the seventh. In John's gospel, which alludes to Genesis, six days lead up to the first manifestation of Jesus' glory.

When we remember that Genesis is part of the context within which we are to understand John's allegory we hear the word "woman" differently. Rather than hearing the word as a rebuff to Mary, we hear it as a reference to the human race. Mary represents the mother of all the living just as Eve, referred to as the "woman" in the book of Genesis, represents the mother of all the living.

In her symbolic role as the mother of all the living, Mary says to Jesus, "They have no wine."

Notice that the setting for the woman's words is a wedding. On the allegorical level, a wedding is a well-known image for the covenant relationship between God and his people. John's audience would have been familiar with this image since it appears in the Old Testament books of Hosea and the Song of Songs, as well as in Jesus' parables which compare the kingdom of God to a wedding feast.

So the mother of all the living is saying about the guests at the wedding—those in the covenant relationship—"They have no wine." They are without spiritual drink.

The story continues. "Now, six stone jars were standing there for the Jewish rites of purification, each holding twenty or thirty gallons" (John 2:6). At an allegorical level the fact that the stone jars are empty represents the empty effect of the Jewish law. A new spiritual order is being initiated and the old law, the old rites of purification, are empty and without effect.

Jesus fills up the empty jars, meant for the Jewish rites of purification, with water which becomes wine. Water and wine are the symbols which we use to this day in our sacraments of new life, our sacraments of initiation. In other words, Jesus replaces the empty rituals of Judaism with baptism and the eucharist. Jesus initiates the new and effective purification rites; Jesus initiates the new spiritual order.

John concludes his allegorical account with the words, "This, the first of his signs, Jesus did at Cana in Galilee, and manifested his glory; and his disciples believed in him" (John 2:11).

The word "signs" is a clear warning to the reader that the literal level of the text is supposed to point to something else. Signs don't exist for themselves but to point to something else.

The "sign" is a manifestation of Jesus' glory. As we read John's gospel we will see that John uses his whole gospel as a vehicle to manifest Jesus' glory. In John's gospel it is as though Jesus' humanity is merely a diaphanous robe through which his divinity shines.

The fact that John constantly pictures Jesus' glory as showing through his humanity is another way in which John is trying to teach his audience. John wants his end of the century audience to understand that the risen, glorified, Jesus is still present to them in his church. Christ is present to them in water and wine. We will see John's focus on Jesus' real presence to his audience through the church occur and reoccur as we continue to read John's gospel.

Review Questions

1. How does John use the event level of his narrative?
2. What does the word "woman" refer to on the allegorical level?
3. What does a wedding stand for on the allegorical level?
4. What does "They have no wine" mean on the allegorical level?
5. What does the water and wine filling empty purification jars mean on the allegorical level?
6. What is John teaching his audience?

Discussion Questions

1. What do you think of the allegorical interpretation given in this article? Do you think it is far-fetched? Reasonable? Explain.

2. When an author wants an audience to interpret something allegorically the author gives the audience a hint by having something "not quite right" on the literal level. Do you think John has given any such hints? What are they?
3. Do you think John's theme—that the risen Christ is powerful and present in and through the church—is true? Do you have any experience to verify this teaching?

ARTICLE 5

The Cleansing of the Temple

Question: "This story about the cleansing of the temple is out of place (John 2:13–18). I thought the cleansing of the temple happened near the end of Jesus' ministry. Why does John place the incident here?"

This is a good question. Notice that the questioner has brought his knowledge of the content of the story of Jesus' life to the text. However, he has not assumed that the fact that the synoptics and John differ on the chronology of the cleansing of the temple should cause us to ask, "Which is accurate historically?" Rather the questioner has asked, "Why does John place the incident here?" The assumption behind the question is that John has a reason for putting the episode here, and that the reason may have nothing to do with the historical order of events. The person who asked this question has the right focus on John's gospel.

The cleansing of the temple comes a few days after the wedding feast at Cana. Notice that the account of this incident begins, "The passover of the Jews was at hand . . ." (John 2:13). Over and over John will mention a Jewish feast as the backdrop for Jesus' activities. The reason for this is that John is emphasizing that the new spiritual order instituted by Jesus is replacing the old order. This is the first mention of the passover. The third will be the day Jesus dies.

Remember that the passover celebration is the Jewish covenant celebration. Any mention of passover is a reference to the relationship between God and his people as understood and celebrated by the Jewish people.

On the literal level, Jesus goes at passover time to the tem-

---

**PASSAGES IN WHICH A JEWISH FESTIVAL IS THE
BACKGROUND OF JESUS' ACTIVITY**

2:23	Passover
4:45	Festival
5:1	Festival
6:4	Passover
7:2ff	Feast of Tabernacles
12:12ff	Festival
13:1	Passover

---

ple and finds it not a place of worship but a "house of trade" (John 2:16).

However, John's message is not to be found on the literal level but on the allegorical level. John makes this perfectly clear in the dialogue which follows: "The Jews then said to him, 'What sign have you to show us for doing this?' Jesus answered them, 'Destroy this temple and in three days I will raise it up.' The Jews then said, 'It has taken forty-six years to build this temple, and will you raise it up in six days?' But he spoke of the temple of his body" (John 2:18–21).

In this interchange John explains his technique. John recounts a story which appears to be about an event (the cleansing of the temple), but is actually about something else entirely (yet to be explained). He then introduces a dialogue in which Jesus speaks metaphorically but is understood literally. The misunderstanding results in Jesus or the narrator correcting the literal misunderstanding and elaborating on the metaphorical significance of what has been said.

The clue to the allegorical level in this instance is the word "temple." As we search for the allegorical level of meaning hidden in the account of the event the narrator tells us that "temple" is not to be understood as the building of brick and mortar but rather as Jesus' body. "But he spoke of the temple of his body" (John 2:21).

For Christians Jesus' body is the church. This metaphor had been well developed by Paul over thirty years before John is writing his gospel. Paul states this most succinctly when he says, "We are the temple of the living God" (2 Corinthians 6:16). But Paul elaborates on the image of the church as the body of Christ in several of his letters. For example, in 1 Corinthians we read, "For just as the body is one and has many members, and all the members of the body, though many, are one body, so it is with Christ. For by one Spirit we were all baptized into one body— Jews or Greeks, slaves or free—and all were made to drink of one spirit. . . . Now you are the body of Christ and individually members of it" (1 Corinthians 12:12–13, 27).

With this clue we can now understand the allegorical level of meaning to the cleansing of the temple, and we can also understand why John places the incident right after the wedding at Cana.

The historical Jesus stands for the risen Christ. The temple stands for the church. Those who are selling oxen and sheep as well as the money changers stand for those who misunderstand the spiritual order, who turn worship into trade, who think that they can earn salvation by obedience to the law. Jesus' anger stands for God's judgment on this misunderstanding. Jesus' driving out the money changers stands for Jesus' cleansing of the "temple," the church. Through the story of the cleansing of the temple John is teaching his end of the century audience that the risen Christ has cleansed his temple, the church. Once we comprehend the allegorical level of the story we can understand John's reasons for placing the story where he does.

The cleansing of the temple is placed after the marriage feast at Cana because the marriage feast is about the new birth available to God's people through baptism and the eucharist. The effect of baptism is the cleansing of the "temple." So the cleansing of the temple comes immediately after the wedding feast at Cana, just as freedom from sin follows baptism.

Many students are astounded by these allegorical interpretations. "You're reading into this!" is a common accusation. However, as we continue to read John's gospel we will find more and more examples of allegory explained by dialogue. As we learn to "translate" the allegory we will begin to probe the spiritual mysteries which John wants his audience to understand.

Review Questions

1. Why does John so consistently use Jewish feasts as the backdrop for Jesus' activities?
2. How does John make it clear to his audience that one should look for an allegorical level of meaning?
3. What is the allegorical significance of the word "temple"?
4. What is the allegorical significance of the cleansing of the temple?
5. Why is the cleansing of the temple placed after the wedding feast at Cana?

Discussion Questions

1. Why is "Why did John place the cleansing of the temple here?" a more useful question than "When exactly did Jesus cleanse the temple?"
2. Do you agree or disagree with the explanation of the allegory in this article? Explain.
3. Do you think people in our society have turned worship into trade? Explain.

ARTICLE 6

Dialogues Explain the Signs

Question: "Nicodemus seems thick-headed. Surely he knew that Jesus didn't expect him to crawl back in his mother's womb when Jesus said, 'Unless one is born anew he cannot see the kingdom of God' (John 3:3). Why does Nicodemus ask, 'How can a man be born when he is old? Can he enter a second time into his mother's womb and be born?' " (John 3:4).

Nicodemus, like many other people whom we will meet in John's gospel (i.e. the woman at the well, the apostles themselves—and perhaps like those who are reading John's gospel) is pictured as too literal in his thinking. John has composed this conversation between Jesus and Nicodemus to illustrate through dialogue the necessity to move beyond the literal and historical in order to understand the spiritual. More specifically, John is using Nicodemus' misunderstanding and Jesus' long dialogue/monologue to explain more clearly the truth which he has already taught allegorically through the first great sign, the wedding feast at Cana.

Let's back up and see how these conclusions have been reached. First, we are suggesting that this dialogue should be read as a composition of John's rather than as a description of an historical event. Perhaps it would be easier to understand John's technique if you pictured his gospel taking place on a stage. On stage, front and center, the events described in the narrative are acted out: the wedding feast at Cana and the cleansing of the temple. On the side, perhaps on a bar stool, sits Jesus. The spotlight shifts to Jesus as commentator. Nicodemus comes out of the

---

METAPHOR

A *metaphor* is a comparison that does not use "like" or "as."

A *simile* is a comparison that uses "like" or "as."

Example of a *simile:* The nurse is like an angel.

Example of a *metaphor:* The nurse is an angel.

---

dark ("by night" means in darkness) into the light which is Jesus. For a short time Jesus and Nicodemus appear to be in a dialogue. However, the dialogue soon turns into a monologue. Nicodemus' question has been a literary technique to allow John to elaborate on his teaching by having Jesus explain at length. Soon the spotlight would no longer include Nicodemus, and the audience would hardly notice his absence. All attention would be on Jesus, the light, and the mystery which he is trying to explain.

Nicodemus serves as an example that one must move beyond the literal and historical in order to understand the spiritual. Nicodemus is stuck at the literal level. When Jesus says, "Unless one is born anew," he is obviously speaking metaphorically. Jesus is not talking about physical birth. He is talking about spiritual life, and in the process of trying to explain what he means he uses the metaphor "birth."

Nicodemus is thinking of the material realm, not the spiritual realm. When he hears the word "birth" he does not understand it as a metaphor but as a literal statement. So he asks, "How can a man be born when he is old? Can he enter a second time in his mother's womb and be born?" (John 3:4).

John's audience, when reading Nicodemus' response, is probably well able to see where Nicodemus is making his mistake, just as the person who asked the original question did. Nicodemus might well seem "thick-headed." However, the person who fails to see the allegorical significance of the events which John has described is being thick-headed in exactly the same way. The dialogue is composed to explain the allegorical significance of the "sign," the manifestation of Jesus' glory which John wants his audience to see shining through the account of the wedding feast at Cana.

John explains through Jesus, "Truly, truly, I say to you, unless one is born of water and the Spirit, he cannot enter the kingdom of God" (John 3:5).

The phrase "born of water and the Spirit" is, of course, a reference to baptism. Baptism is the Christian initiation rite, the birth into Christ's body, the church. John the Baptist, in his witness to Christ in the first chapter of this gospel, refers to this baptism by the Spirit. "I saw the Spirit descend as a dove from heaven, and it remained on him (Jesus). I myself did not know him, but he who sent me to baptize with water said to me, 'He on whom you see the Spirit descend and remain, this is he who baptizes with the Holy Spirit' " (John 1:32–33).

In Nicodemus' response to Jesus' words, Nicodemus has become a symbol for the unbelieving Jews. "Nicodemus said to him, 'How can this be?' Jesus answered him, 'Are you a teacher of Israel, and yet you do not understand this?' " (John 3:9–10). John thus has Jesus continue to explain the core of John's message to believers and non-believers alike. "For God so loved the world that he gave his only Son, that whoever believes in him should not perish but have eternal life" (John 3:16). Baptism is birth into this eternal life.

In the dialogue with Nicodemus, then, we hear Jesus explain what John already taught through his symbolic account of water and wine filling the empty Jewish purification jars at the wedding of Cana. The old ways have been replaced. Jesus, God's Son, has initiated a new spiritual order. One must be born again, be baptized, to belong to the new covenant community, the church, and so enter the kingdom and eternal life.

Review Questions

1. In what way might Nicodemus' misunderstanding be described as a "literary technique"?
2. What problem in thinking does Nicodemus have?
3. What function does the dialogue/monologue with Nicodemus have?
4. What is the core of John's message in this dialogue/monologue?
5. What does "born again" mean?

Discussion Questions

1. Why do you think baptism is referred to as being "born of water and the Spirit"?
2. What advantage is there for the author of this gospel to have Jesus in dialogue with people who consistently take his metaphors literally?
3. When do you think you are born into eternal life? Why do you think this?

ARTICLE 7

"The Jews" in John's Gospel

Question: "Both Jesus and John seem to judge harshly those who don't believe in Jesus (John 3:18–21; 3:36). How can people be expected to believe so quickly?"

Before we answer this question we must correct a false presumption which lies behind it. The questioner is correct in noting that both Jesus and John are pictured as judging harshly those who don't believe in Jesus. At the end of his dialogue/monologue with Nicodemus Jesus is pictured as saying, "He who believes in him (i.e. God's Son) is not condemned; he who does not believe is condemned already, because he has not believed in the name of the only Son of God. And this is the judgment, that the light has come into the world, and men loved darkness rather than light, because their deeds were evil. For every one who does evil hated the light, and does not come to the light, lest his deeds should be exposed" (John 3:18–20).

Later in the same chapter John is pictured as saying, "He who believes in the Son has eternal life; he who does not obey the Son shall not see life, but the wrath of God rests upon him" (John 3:36).

However, when the questioner then asks "How can people be expected to believe so quickly?" the questioner is assuming that she is reading an account that guarantees historical accuracy and historical chronology. This presumption is wrong. John is not trying to give an accurate picture of historical events and relationships. He is counting on his audience already knowing the basic story. Rather, he is using that story to teach his end of the century audience the spiritual realities of their own lives as those realities have been revealed through Jesus Christ.

At the time John is writing, bitter feelings had developed between those Jews who followed Jesus and those Jews who did not. Remember that Jesus, his family, and his original disciples were all Jewish. So in the earliest days, to be Jewish and to be Christian were compatible. As time went on both Jews and Gentiles became Christian. While it was not necessary to become Jewish to become Christian, neither did one have to separate oneself from Judaism in order to become Christian. One could be both Jewish and Christian.

However, by the time John was writing, Jews who did not accept Christ viewed those Jews who did accept Christ as committing blasphemy because of their belief that Jesus and the Father are, in some sense, one.

Because this belief was regarded as blasphemous by many Jews, those Jews who believed in Christ were being expelled from the synagogue. Jewish Christians, therefore, felt persecuted by the Jews who were not Christian.

The undertone of hostility between those who believed in Jesus and "the Jews" who were persecuting Jewish Christians is evident throughout John's gospel. In addition to the two instances noted by the questioner you will notice other examples of harsh judgment on the unbelieving "Jews."

Since John's intent is not to teach at the historical level, but to use the historical level to teach allegorically about the spiritual realities in the life of his audience, John sometimes introduces a detail into his narrative which is not historically consistent with the setting of the story—the time of Jesus' life on earth.

For instance, even though Jews were not expelled from the synagogue for embracing Christianity during Jesus' lifetime, the fact that Jews are being expelled appears several times. In the story of the cure of the blind man we read: "The Jews did not believe that he had been blind and had received his sight, until they called the parents of the man who had received his sight, and asked them 'Is this your son, who you say was born blind? How then does he now see?' His parents answered, 'We know that this is our son, and that he was born blind, but how he now sees we do not know, nor do we know who opened his eyes, Ask him; he is of age; he will speak for himself.' His parents said this because they feared the Jews, for the Jews had already agreed that if any one should confess him to be Christ, he was to be put out of the synagogue. Therefore his parents said, 'He is of age, ask him' " (John 9:18–23).

Again in chapter 12 the narrator's voice tells us: "Nevertheless many even of the authorities believed in him, but for fear of the Pharisees they did not confess it, lest they should be put out of the synagogue: for they loved the praise of men more than the praise of God" (John 12:42).

These references do not accurately reflect the time of Jesus, but they do accurately reflect the time of John's audience.

This same lack of historical intent is present in John's use of the words "the Jews." The author of John's gospel uses the words "the Jews" to refer to those who oppose and refuse to believe in Jesus Christ. Such a designation would, of course, have been historically inaccurate on Jesus' lips.

The whole tone of condemnation of "the Jews" in John's gospel reflects the attitude of the author of the gospel toward those who opposed Christians at the time he is writing. This tone does not reflect Jesus' attitude toward the Jews in his own life-time, nor does it reflect the attitude a modern day Christian should have toward Jews.

Jesus did not condemn those who failed to believe in him immediately. If he had, all of the apostles would have been among the condemned. These harsh words are John's judgment on his contemporary adversaries, the "Jews," who are persecuting his Christian audience.

Review Questions

1. What false presumption lies behind the question which begins this article?
2. What is the relationship between "the Jews" and Christians by the time John is writing?
3. What belief of the Christians caused the Jews to persecute them?
4. What detail in John's gospel is inconsistent with Jesus' time but not inconsistent with the time of John and his audience?

5. What does this inconsistency tell us about the way we should interpret the attitude toward "the Jews" in this gospel?

Discussion Questions

1. Would you call the author of this gospel antisemitic? Why or why not?
2. If you read a story in which George Washington watched television, what conclusion would you draw about the historicity of the account? What does this question have to do with the question at the beginning of this article?
3. Do you expect to see anyone who didn't believe in Christ in heaven? Why or why not?

ARTICLE 8

The Samaritan Woman
and Living Water

Question: "Why did Jesus start talking to the Samaritan woman about 'living water'? Didn't he know she would not be able to understand him?"

As is constantly true in John's gospel, we must remember to ask, "What is John teaching his audience through this account?" This question will often lead us to understand John's gospel better than if we ask only, "What is Jesus saying to his audience?" We need to ask both of these questions.

With this in mind, let us reword the question. Instead of asking "Why did Jesus start talking to the Samaritan woman about living water?" we will start by asking "What is John teaching his audience as he pictures Jesus talking to the Samaritan woman about living water?"

The conversation between Jesus and the Samaritan woman follows the pattern we have already noted in the conversation between Jesus and Nicodemus. Jesus speaks metaphorically. His listener understands him literally. This literal misunderstanding gives Jesus (and John) the opportunity to elaborate on the metaphor, to teach the spiritual truth more clearly.

The conversation starts with Jesus asking the woman for a drink. The woman is completely taken aback by Jesus' request because it is most unusual for a man to speak to a woman in public, much less for a Jewish man to speak to a Samaritan woman. Remember, Jews considered Samaritans unclean and did not associate with them. It is at this point that Jesus begins to speak metaphorically. He says, "If you knew the gift of God, and who it is that is saying to you, 'Give me a drink,' you would have asked him, and he would have given you living water" (John 4:10).

The woman understands the word "water" as referring to physical water, just as Nicodemus understood the word "birth" to refer to physical birth. Jesus is using the word "water" as a metaphor. The Samaritan woman reveals her misunderstanding when she says, "Sir, you have nothing to draw with, and the well is deep; where do you get that living water?" (John 4:11).

The misunderstanding proceeds as Jesus continues to speak metaphorically and the woman continues to understand him literally. " 'But whoever drinks of the water that I shall give him will become in him a spring of water welling up to eternal life.' The woman said to him, 'Sir, give me this water that I may not thirst, nor come here to draw' " (John 4:14–15).

One cannot read this story without taking delight in the personality of the Samaritan woman. She is anything but a shrinking violet. One might expect her to withdraw from the conversation when Jesus refers to her five husbands, and the fact that the man with whom she now lives is not her husband. As we hear this history we suddenly realize why the woman came to the well by herself at noon rather than with the other women. This woman was an outcast in her society. She was hungry for love and truly did long for living water.

Instead of shrinking away in shame at Jesus' words the Samaritan woman rather feistily changes the subject. "Our fathers worshiped on this mountain; and you say that Jerusalem is the place where men ought to worship" (John 4:29).

In Jesus' reply we can hear John defending those Jewish Christians who had been expelled from the synagogue: "Woman, believe me, the hour is coming when neither on this mountain nor in Jerusalem will you worship the Father. You worship what you do not know; we worship what we know, for salvation is from the Jews. But the hour is coming, and now is, when the true worshipers will worship the Father in spirit and truth, for such the Father seeks to worship him. God is spirit and truth" (John 4:21–24).

The conversation then moves to the identity of Jesus as the messiah, the question central to John's gospel. "The woman said to him, 'I know that the messiah is coming (he who is called Christ); when he comes, he will show us all things.' Jesus said to her, 'I who speak to you am he' " (John 25:26).

The woman rushes back to town to tell the people, a very unusual act on her part since she was not admired by the townspeople.

Next the disciples arrive. The author of John's gospel uses exactly the same technique in the dialogue between Jesus and the disciples as he had used with the Samaritan woman and with Nicodemus. Jesus speaks metaphorically but he is understood literally. This misunderstanding allows Jesus (and John) to elaborate. "Meanwhile the disciples besought him, saying, 'Rabbi, eat.' But he said to them, 'I have food to eat of which you do not know.' So the disciples said to one another, 'Has any one brought him food?' Jesus said to them, 'My food is to do the will of him who sent me, and to accomplish his work' " (John 4:31–34).

John concludes his account by showing how the townspeople came to believe. Many had believed simply on the witness of the woman, an astounding detail since a woman's testimony was not considered reliable and would not, by itself, have carried any weight in judicial proceedings. This initial belief resulted in the people asking Jesus to stay with them. Jesus does, and the people come to believe not on the witness of another but from their own experience.

In this story John is teaching his audience that they too must learn to think metaphorically in order to understand spiritual realities. They must understand, as did the Samaritan woman and her townspeople, that Jesus Christ is the savior of the world. In addition their belief should rest not just on the testimony of others, those earlier Christians who had known Jesus during his life on earth, but on their own experience of Christ in the living water, of their own union with Christ and his church in baptism. John's readers should come to recognize that they have received from Christ that living water which "will turn into a spring inside them, welling up to eternal life" (John 4:14).

Review Questions

1. What two questions should we always ask ourselves when reading John's gospel?
2. What pattern is evident in the conversation between Jesus and the Samaritan woman?
3. What question, central to John's gospel, does Jesus discuss with the Samaritan woman?
4. What about the townspeople's belief does John think should be true of his audience's belief too?

Discussion Questions

1. What is unusual about Jesus' talking to the Samaritan woman? About her being a witness to her townspeople? Are there some people in our society whom you would be slow to believe? Who? Why?
2. Do you agree that one can hear John defending those Christian Jews who have been expelled from the synagogue in Jesus' answer to the Samaritan woman about the proper place for worship? Why or why not?
3. Why do you think the disciples are surprised at Jesus' actions and words?
4. Are there any expectations in our society which you think should be disobeyed rather than obeyed? What are they?

ARTICLE 9

Unless You See Signs and Wonders?

Question: "Why did Jesus say 'Unless you see signs and wonders you will not believe' (John 4:48) to the man who asked that his son be healed? The man must have had faith or he wouldn't have asked."

As we mentioned in our explanation of Jesus' first sign at Cana, the wedding feast at which Jesus addressed his mother as "woman," it is important to notice any inconsistency or any jarring detail in the literal level of an account that is to be read allegorically. The reason for this is that the inconsistency is often a clue to the author's purpose.

In addition we must remember that in John's gospel the conversation between Jesus and his audience is often better understood if one thinks of the words as being addressed to John's end of the century audience by the risen Christ rather than to the person pictured as physically present to the historical Jesus. We will need to draw on both of these insights to answer this question.

The questioner's sense that Jesus' words seem a little strange is exactly on target. Why would Jesus accuse the man of lacking faith unless he sees signs and portents? Obviously the man has faith or he would not have asked Jesus to come to cure his son.

However, the words might be more appropriate if addressed to John's audience. John's audience was living some fifty to sixty years after Jesus' life on earth. As was already discussed, Jesus' followers expected him to return imminently. Now that half a century has passed, John's audience might well be thinking, "Those Christians who lived at the time Jesus lived were the

fortunate ones. They were alive to experience Jesus' healing power."

The point of John's gospel is to teach his audience that Jesus is
just as present to them in his church and in what we have come
to call the sacraments as he was present to his contemporaries.
The purpose of this particular episode is to emphasize that Jesus
need not be physically present in order for a person of faith to
experience his healing power.

Notice that the man who asked Jesus to cure his son asked
Jesus to "come." Jesus did not come. He simply said, "Go, your
son will live" (John 4:49). The man believed Jesus and went
home, to discover that his son had been healed at the very time
when Jesus had said, "Your son will live."

The author tells us, "This was now the second sign that Jesus
did when he had come from Judea to Galilee" (John 4:54). We
know that the signs in John's gospel are to be interpreted allegorically and that the same teaching which appears in the allegorical interpretation will also appear in a dialogue.

In this allegory the historical Jesus stands for the risen Christ.
The court official whose son was sick stands for those in John's
audience who believe in Jesus but who want Jesus to "come,"
who feel that the lack of Jesus' physical presence separates them
from experiencing Christ's healing power. The fact that the son
is healed stands for the fact that no one who has faith is separated
from Christ's power by mere physical distance. John's audience
can and should know of Christ's power and presence from their
own experience and not just from the witness of previous generations.

If you remember, this same point was made in the story which
we just read about the Samaritan woman at the well. When Jesus
was speaking to the woman about living water he was actually
speaking to her about baptism. Later in the story we noted that
her townsfolk came to believe in Jesus not just from her testimony but from their own experience.

This is what John wants to teach his audience. They have
"drunk" of the "waters of eternal life" through baptism (the first
sign at Cana: the wedding feast). They now walk with Christ in

faith (the second sign at Cana: the cure of the nobleman's son). Even though they do not experience Jesus' physical presence they can nonetheless experience Christ's saving power.

Review Questions

1. Why is it important to notice any inconsistency in the literal level of a story that is meant to be interpreted allegorically?
2. What attitude might John's audience have had toward those who lived at the time of Jesus?
3. To whom are the words "So you won't believe unless you see signs and portents" actually addressed on the allegorical level?
4. What is John teaching in this second sign?

Discussion Questions

1. Do you envy Jesus' contemporaries? Why or why not?
2. Do you believe Christ's healing power is still present? Why or why not?
3. Do you agree with the allegorical interpretation given of this second sign? Why or why not?

ARTICLE 10

The Risen Christ Can Forgive Sin

Question: "Why does Jesus say to the man cured in the pool at Bethzatha, 'See, you are well! Sin no more, that nothing worse befall you' (John 5:14). Is Jesus saying that the man's sickness was a punishment for sin?"

Jesus does not teach that physical illness is a punishment for sin. The belief that suffering was punishment for sin, and thus deserved, was held by many of Jesus' contemporaries. That many believed this is clearly reflected by a question which Jesus' disciples are pictured as asking him a little later in John's gospel: "Rabbi, who sinned, this man or his parents, that he was born blind?" (John 9:1).

Jesus does not let this belief go unchallenged, for he responds, "It was not that this man sinned, or his parents, but that the works of God might be made manifest in him" (John 9:2).

If Jesus is not saying that illness is punishment for sin, what is he saying?

Since this remark of Jesus' appears in the account of the third sign which Jesus performs in John's gospel we should look for the answer to the question at the allegorical level. All the signs are to be interpreted allegorically.

While sickness is not punishment for sin, sickness works very well as a symbol for sin in an allegory. At the allegorical level, to heal physically would stand for healing spiritually—forgiving sin.

It is interesting to note that while John does picture Jesus healing people of physical ailments he does not picture Jesus performing exorcisms. Scholars suggest that this is because physical healing would have had an obvious allegorical significance in the minds of John's audience while exorcisms would not. Since people thought that sickness was punishment for sin, to be healed of sickness would indicate that sin had been forgiven. Possession was not considered punishment for sin and so exorcisms would lack such an allegorical significance.

Jesus' words, "See, you are well! Sin no more, that nothing worse befall you" (John 5:14), will be more understandable after we interpret the account of this sign as an allegory.

The facts that "there was a Jewish festival" (John 5:1) and that the waters of the Sheep Pool have not been accessible stand for the fact that Jewish feasts and practices are ineffective and are being replaced. The ill man stands for a person in need of forgiveness.

While the ill man had no one to take him to the waters of the Sheep Pool for healing, John's audience does: in Christ and his church. The first sign (the wedding at Cana) symbolized this new birth. The second sign (the cure of the nobleman's son) symbolized the faith necessary for the spiritual journey. This third sign symbolizes Christ's ever present healing power, the power to forgive sin, which is present in baptism and which accompanies us on the journey.

As the story continues the dialogue turns to an explicit conversation about sin. The Pharisees think both the man and Jesus have sinned: the man by carrying his pallet on the sabbath, and Jesus by curing on the sabbath. This accusation gives Jesus the opportunity to say in dialogue what the third sign has taught allegorically. "The Father judges no one, but has given all judgment to the Son" (John 5:22). In other words, the risen Christ can still forgive sin.

Now that we understand the allegorical significance of the third sign we can better understand Jesus' words, "See, you are well! Sin no more, that nothing worse befall you" (John 5:14). Again we should picture the words as addressed to John's audience by the risen Christ. Now that they have been reborn they should be careful not to fall back into their old sinful ways or they will be in worse shape spiritually than they were before.

They need not live in fear, though, because Christ has the power to forgive sin.

Review Questions

1. Does Jesus teach that physical suffering is punishment for sin? What evidence do you have to support your answer?
2. How do scholars account for the fact that there are no exorcisms in John's gospel?
3. What is John teaching his audience through the allegorical message contained in this third sign?
4. What dialogue confirms this allegorical interpretation?
5. How would you answer the question with which this article began?

Discussion Questions

1. Do you think people today still think of suffering as punishment for sin? Why or why not?
2. Do you believe the risen Christ still has power to forgive sin? How might you experience that forgiveness?
3. If you think of the ill man as standing for a person in need of forgiveness, do Jesus' words of warning about not falling back into sin make sense to you? Why or why not?

ARTICLE 11

The Risen Christ Feeds His People

Question: "The multiplication of the loaves is different in John's gospel than it was in the synoptics. In the synoptics you said that the story might not be a miracle story at all, but here it seems to be. Is this right?"

The person who asked this question is a careful reader. She has correctly noted that there are some subtle differences in this account as compared to the accounts we read in Mark (Mark 6:31–44; 8:1–10), Matthew (Matthew 14:13–21; 15:32–38), and Luke (Luke 9:10–17). What are the differences? In the synoptics we pointed out that Jesus gave the bread to his disciples to distribute. Here he distributes it himself. In several of the synoptic accounts we saw that Jesus "blessed and broke" the bread. Here Jesus "gives thanks." In the synoptics we noted that the crowd did not marvel, as one would expect in a miracle story. Here, "when the people saw the sign which he had done, they said, 'This is indeed the prophet who is to come into the world' " (John 6:14). What is the significance of these differences? Is the main motive behind this story to tell of a miracle?

Notice that John persists in using the word "sign," not "miracle." Whenever we hear John describe an action of Jesus with that word, we know that we are to look for an allegorical level of meaning in the account. We can also expect a dialogue to explain the allegorical significance of the sign.

An allegory is a different kind of writing than a miracle story. If we regard this account as a simple miracle story, and so do not look for a level of meaning deeper than the literal level, we will fail to understand what John hopes to teach.

So let us interpret the story as an allegory. "Now the passover, the feast of the Jews, was at hand" (John 6:4). Once again a Jewish feast is being replaced. Also, once again, the historical Jesus in the account stands for the risen Christ. The disciples stand for the church. The crowd stands for those hungry for spiritual nourishment.

Jesus himself distributes the bread because Jesus is the bread of life. It is he who satisfies our hunger.

Jesus "gives thanks." The Greek (the original language of the gospel) word for "thanks" is *eucharisteo*. This gives us the clue that the bread in this allegory stands for the eucharist.

Through this allegory John is teaching his audience that Christ is present to them in the eucharist just as surely as the historical Jesus was present to his contemporaries. Christ is still able to feed his people.

This lesson is reaffirmed in the dialogue which follows only a few verses later. The people who had been fed tried to track Jesus down. When they found him Jesus says, "Truly, truly, I say to you, you seek me, not because you saw signs, but because you ate your fill of the loaves. Do not labor for the food which perishes, but for the food which endures to eternal life, which the Son of Man will give to you; for on him has God the Father set his seal" (John 6:26–27).

John too wants his audience to realize that the risen Christ offers them "food" that endures to eternal life.

In this fourth sign we see the next step in the spiritual journey. We have moved from birth in baptism (wedding at Cana) to faith in Christ's power and presence (cure of the nobleman's son) to forgiveness of sins (cure of the man at the Sheep Pool) to food for the journey—the eucharist (multiplication of the loaves). That John intends us to understand this account allegorically is made even more evident as he pictures Jesus saying, "I am the bread of life; he who comes to me shall not hunger, and he who believes in me shall never thirst" (John 6:35). John's audience, too, will never be hungry if they stay close to Christ through the eucharist.

Review Questions

1. How does John's "multiplication of the loaves" differ from the accounts in the synoptic gospels?
2. What is John teaching at the allegorical level in his "multiplication of the loaves"? Explain.
3. What dialogue confirms this allegorical interpretation?

Discussion Questions

1. What does it mean to say that Jesus is the bread of life?
2. Do you have access to the bread of life? How?
3. Do you agree with the allegorical interpretation given this fourth sign? Why or why not?

ARTICLE 12

The Risen Christ Says,
"I Am with You"

Question: "I'm afraid I'm just missing the point when it comes to Jesus' walking on the water (John 6:16–24). This story seems very strange on the literal level, and I can't find any allegorical significance either. What's up?"

The person who asked this question has caught on to the method necessary in order to understand John. To ask "What is the allegorical significance?" is to ask the right question.

The account of Jesus' walking on the water is placed between the multiplication of the loaves and the dialogue which explains its allegorical meaning. Immediately after the multiplication of the loaves Jesus went to the hills by himself.

Without Jesus the disciples went down to the shore. The narrator comments, "It was now dark and Jesus had not yet come to them" (John 6:16). As with Nicodemus, when someone is separated from Jesus, that person is "in the dark." Also, without Jesus, the way is rough: "The sea rose because a strong wind was blowing" (John 6:19).

This scene allegorically pictures Jesus' disciples in the same situation in which John's audience finds itself. Jesus had been with his people. However, he had gone, and had not as yet rejoined them. They are feeling the separation.

As the story continues, the disciples see Jesus walking on the lake and coming toward the boat. They are frightened. They, of course, did not expect to be reunited with Jesus until they had reached their destination. To have Jesus present "en route" was something they didn't realize was possible.

Jesus says, "It is I. Do not be afraid" (John 6:20). The words "It is I" do not hit our ears as they would have hit the ears of John's audience. The Greek for "It is I" is *ego eimi*. The words are correctly translated "It is I," but they have an additional and very important meaning to John's audience.

You are perhaps familiar with the story of how God appeared to Moses in the burning bush (see Exodus 3:1–23). In that account Moses says to God: "If I come to the people of Israel and say to them, 'The God of your fathers has sent me to you,' and they ask me, 'What is his name?' What shall I say to them?" God said to Moses, "I AM who I AM." And he said, "Say this to the people of Israel. 'I AM has sent me to you' " (Exodus 3:13–14).

Some two hundred and fifty years before Jesus' life on earth, the Old Testament was translated into Greek. This Greek translation is called the Septuagint. In the Septuagint, the Greek words used to translate, "I AM," in "I AM has sent me to you," are *ego eimi*. The words name God.

So when John's audience read the account of Jesus walking on the water and saying "*ego eimi*," they realize that John is identifying Jesus with God.

John has made this claim throughout his gospel. We saw it in the prologue which begins, "In the beginning was the Word, and the Word was with God, and the Word was God" (John 1:1). We saw it in Jesus' words to the woman at the well when he said: "I who speak to you am he" (John 4:26). We saw it in the dialogue/monologue which followed the cure of the man at the Sheep Pool. Jesus said to the Jews, " 'My Father is working still, and I am working.' This was why the Jews sought all the more to kill him because he not only broke the sabbath but also called God his own Father, making himself equal to God" (John 5:18).

As you continue to read John's gospel you will see other instances in which Jesus says "It is I" or "I am he." When you read these words on Jesus' lips remember that not only "the Jews" in John's account, but "the Jews" in John's audience, hear the words as blasphemous because they hear both Jesus and John identifying Jesus with Yahweh.

However, the disciples in the boat who hear Jesus say, "It is I,

---

SOME "I AM," "IT IS I," AND "I AM . . ." PASSAGES IN JOHN'S GOSPEL

4:26   "I am he."
6:20   "It is I. Do not be afraid."
6:35   "I am the bread of life."
8:12   "I am the light of the world."
8:24   "I am he."
8:28   "I am he."
8:58   "I AM."
10:7   "I am the gate of the sheepfold."
10:11 "I am the good shepherd."
10:36 "I am the Son of God."
11:25 "I am the resurrection."
13:13 "So I am."
13:19 "I am he."
14:6   "I am the way, the truth and the life."
15:1   "I am the true vine."
18:6   "I am he."
18:8   "I am he."
18:37 "I am a king."

---

do not be afraid," are glad. "Then they were glad to take him into the boat, and immediately the boat was at the land to which they were going" (John 6:21).

Through this fifth sign John is teaching his audience that even though Christ may appear to be temporarily absent, he is actually still with them. No situation can separate them from the risen Christ. They are never left alone on life's journey.

The allegorical significance of this sign is re-emphasized in the dialogue/monologue at the last supper when Jesus tells his apostles: "I will not leave you desolate. I will come to you. Yet a little while and the world will see me no more, but you will see me; because I live, you will live also" (John 14:18–19).

John wants his audience to know that they too live in the presence and power of the risen Christ.

Review Questions

1. If one interprets Jesus' walking on the water allegorically, what does John's audience have in common with the disciples in the boat?
2. What would John's audience have understood by Jesus' words "It is I"?
3. What is the Septuagint?
4. Why would "the Jews" in John's audience have been so upset by reading an account in which Jesus says, "It is I"?
5. What is John teaching his audience through this fifth sign?

Discussion Questions

1. Can you think of any circumstances in which you would be separated from Christ's love and power? Explain.
2. What do you think the author means on the allegorical level by saying, "immediately the boat was at the land to which they were going" (John 6:21)?
3. If you believed what John teaches in this fifth sign, what difference would it make in your day-to-day life?

ARTICLE 13

Where Did Jesus Come From?
Where Is He Going?

Question: "In chapter 7 Jesus tells his brothers that he is not going up to the festival (John 7:8); later he sneaks up (John 7:10), and then he preaches openly (John 7:13). This seems like very strange behavior. Did Jesus just keep changing his mind?"

Whenever something seems incongruous on the literal level in John's gospel we know that we must look for an allegorical meaning. John expects his readers to notice not only that Jesus came up to the festival in secret, and that he preached openly on several occasions, but that he finally left the temple in secret too. "So they took up stones to throw at him; but Jesus hid himself, and went out of the temple" (John 8:59).

These actions, on an allegorical level, relate to the conversations in chapters 7 and 8 about where Jesus came from and where he is going. The conversations are actually about Jesus' identity. Let us look at the conversations in Chapters 7 and 8 in order to demonstrate the truth of these conclusions.

In chapter 7 we read: "Some of the people of Jerusalem said, 'Is not this the man whom they seek to kill? And here he is speaking openly and they say nothing to him! Can it be that the authorities really know that this is the Christ? Yet we know where this man came from; and when the Christ appears no one will know where he comes from.' So Jesus proclaimed as he taught in the temple, 'You know me and you know where I came from. But I have not come of my own accord; he who sent me is true, and him you do not know. I know him for I came from him, and he sent me' " (John 7:23–29).

Soon Jesus adds, "I shall be with you a little longer, and then I go to him who sent me; you will seek me and you will not find me; where I am you cannot come" (John 7:33–34).

A little later in chapter 7 we read: "When they heard these words, some of the people said, 'This is really the prophet.' Others said, 'This is the Christ.' But some said, 'Is the Christ to come from Galilee? Has not scripture said that the Christ is descended from David, and comes from Bethlehem, the village where David was?' So there was a division among the people over him" (John 7:40–43).

You notice in these conversations that the people are discussing Jesus' identity. Is he a prophet? Is he the Christ?

In order to answer the question for themselves they consider Jesus' origin. They think they know that Jesus is from Galilee. This makes it unlikely that Jesus is the Christ because the Christ should be from Bethlehem.

Of course, John's audience knows perfectly well that Jesus is from Bethlehem. When the people say, "We know where he is from," John's audience can see the irony in the fact that, in fact, they don't know that Jesus is from Bethlehem.

However, there is an even deeper irony in these passages. Jesus is the Christ not because he is from Bethlehem but because he is from God, from above. In these chapters John is insisting on Jesus' divinity.

That is why Jesus says, "I know him (God) for I come from him, and he sent me" (John 7:29). This is the claim which we saw in the prologue. Jesus is the pre-existent Word who came from God. This is the claim which John pictures as infuriating "the Jews," the claim which is infuriating John's Jewish contemporaries and is resulting in Christian Jews being expelled from the synagogue.

The dialogue in chapters 7 and 8 states and restates the claim that Jesus is divine because he is from above. The crowd gets progressively abusive. Finally Jesus says, "Truly, truly, I say to you, before Abraham was, I am" (John 8:59). Once again, "I am" is on Jesus' lips, words which name God. In this claim we have the central message of John's gospel.

In the light of these conversations we can see why John pictures Jesus sneaking up to the temple, preaching openly, and sneaking away. These actions symbolize the mysterious truth of Jesus' ministry and Jesus' identity. Jesus' contemporaries heard him preach, but they did not know where he came from or where he was going. They did not recognize Christ's divinity. John's gospel is meant to teach his audience that Christ is truly divine, that he came from God and returned to God.

Review Questions

1. Why are the Jews discussing where Jesus came from?
2. What is ironic about their saying, "We know where you came from"?
3. What is the core claim John is making in chapters 7 and 8 which infuriates the Jews?
4. At an allegorical level, why does John picture Jesus sneaking into town, preaching openly, and sneaking out?

Discussion Questions

1. The Jews were infuriated by John's teaching. Do you hear things taught now that infuriate or annoy you? What are they?
2. How do you understand the relationship between God the Father and Jesus Christ? Explain as best you can.
3. Why is one's answer to this question important if one considers oneself Christian? Do you agree that this is a core issue?

The Man Born Blind
Sees the Light of the World

Question: "It seems that the man born blind was cured without even knowing who Jesus was. Isn't faith necessary for healing?" (John 9:1–14; John 5:1–16; 8:31 also discussed)

This question seems to have been asked by a person who formed expectations from reading the miracle stories in the synoptic gospels and expects to find similar stories in John.

The identical question could have been asked in regard to the cure of the man at the Sheep Pool (John 5:1–16). This man not only lacked faith, but the gospel does not mention that he ever came to faith.

It is true that some of John's "mighty signs" appear, on the surface level, to be similar to episodes in the synoptics (i.e. the multiplication of the loaves, the walking on water). On the other hand, some are unique to John (i.e. the wedding at Cana, the raising of Lazarus). Even when one of John's mighty signs is also present in the synoptics, John does not tell the story for the same reason for which it appears in another gospel. In John's gospel the surface level is always suggesting an allegorical level. The allegorical level is the point of the story.

In the story of the man born blind we have the story of a man who, by progressive steps, grows in his faith. In "the Jews" we have the story of people progressively hardening their hearts.

We will trace the progressive steps in each case, but first I would like to point out how this story might have affected John's audience.

We have already mentioned that one of John's purposes is to

affirm the divinity of Christ in the face of "the Jews" who consider such a claim blasphemous.

You may have noticed when you read chapter 8 that one of those many acrimonious conversations was between Jesus and "the Jews who believed in him" (John 8:31). These very "Jews who believe" are pictured as wanting to kill Jesus. How could this be?

This leads us to the question, "What does it mean to believe in Jesus?" Perhaps a person who thought Jesus was a wise teacher or a miracle worker might claim belief. Perhaps one who saw Jesus as a great prophet might claim belief. Does "to believe in Jesus" demand that one claim that Jesus is divine? To claim that Jesus is divine meant expulsion from the synagogue and perhaps terrible danger. This is because one involved in Jewish worship was excused from participating in Roman pagan worship. Jewish Christians who were expelled from the synagogue would be expected to participate in pagan worship and would face death for refusing to participate. Many died in just this way.

In the story of the blind man we see spelled out the progressive steps of faith. The first statement which the man makes is, "The man called Jesus made clay and anointed my eyes and said to me, 'Go to Siloam and wash;' so I went and washed and received my sight" (John 9:11). At this point the man knows only that the man named Jesus healed his blindness.

The Pharisees then argue about whether a man who cures on the sabbath could be from God. They ask the man, " 'What do you say about him, since he opened your eyes?' He said, 'He is prophet' " (John 9:17).

After talking to the blind man's parents the Jews again argue with the blind man over Jesus' identity. The blind man says, "Why, this is a marvel. You do not know where he comes from, and yet he opened my eyes. We know that God does not listen to sinners, but if anyone is a worshiper of God and does his will, God listens to him. Never since the world began has it been heard that anyone opened the eyes of a man born blind. If this man were not from God, he could do nothing" (John 9:30–33). The man has reasoned his way to an understanding that Jesus must be from God.

Finally Jesus asks the man, " 'Do you believe in the Son of Man?' He answered, 'And who is he, sir, that I may believe in him?' Jesus said to him, 'You have seen him, and it is he who speaks to you.' He said, 'Lord, I believe'; and he worshiped him" (John 9:35–38). To "worship" Jesus is to acknowledge that Jesus is divine. The man grows through all the gradations of belief: "he opened my eyes," "he is a prophet," "he is from God," until he understands Jesus' divinity and thus worships him.

The Jews, on the other hand, progress in the opposite direction. They start with an experience—they see a man who was once blind and can now see. They ask how the man's eyes were opened.

However, as they try to impose their preconceived beliefs on this experience they start to deny the experience rather than question their beliefs. "Since the cure is on the sabbath this man can't be from God." "Perhaps the man was never blind to begin with." "The blind man can't teach us anything since he has obviously been a sinner since birth."

While the blind man comes to see the light of Christ, the Jews become blind. Jesus remarks on this very fact when he says, "For judgment I came into the world, that those who do not see may see, and that those who see may become blind" (John 9:39).

The author gives us the information we need to understand the allegorical level of this mighty sign in Jesus' words just before he heals the blind man. "We must do the works of him who sent me, while it is day; night comes when no one can work. As long as I am in the world, I am the light of the world" (John 9:4–5).

Through this sixth mighty sign John is teaching his audience that they must believe in Christ's divinity and keep their minds and hearts set on Christ, the light of the world.

Review Questions

1. Even if it is a story about the same "miracle," how does a story of a mighty sign in John differ from a miracle story in the synoptic gospels?

2. Why did being expelled from the synagogue result in real danger?
3. Describe the progressive steps in faith experienced by the man who had been blind.
4. Describe the progressive steps in hardening one's heart as illustrated by the Jews.
5. What is John teaching his audience through this sixth mighty sign?

Discussion Questions

1. Have you experienced "steps in a process" in terms of your own faith? Explain.
2. Have you observed ways in which people in our society "harden their hearts" and refuse to deal with reality? What are they?
3. Have you ever had an experience which forced you to examine and modify a belief? Explain.

ARTICLE 15

Death Is Not Death

Question: "Why didn't Jesus go to Lazarus immediately instead of waiting? Then he would have saved Martha and Mary all that grief." (John 11:6–44)

The author of John's gospel wants you to ask this very question. First he tells the story in such a way that the reader is forced to notice Jesus' lack of immediate response: "Now Jesus loved Martha and her sister and Lazarus, so when he heard that he was ill, he stayed two days longer in the place where he was" (John 11:15). One would expect to read, "Now Jesus loved them so he rushed right to them."

In addition the author highlights the question by having both Martha and Mary reproach Jesus for not coming sooner. Martha says, "Lord, if you had been here my brother would not have died" (John 11:21). When Mary sees Jesus she says exactly the same thing. "Lord, if you had been here my brother would not have died" (John 11:32).

The author has Jesus himself answer the question when he pictures him saying to his disciples, " 'Our friend Lazarus has fallen asleep, but I go to awake him out of sleep.' The disciples said to him, 'Lord, if he has fallen asleep he will recover.' Now Jesus had spoken of his death, but they thought that he meant taking rest in sleep. Then Jesus told them plainly, 'Lazarus is dead, and for your sake I am glad that I was not there, so that you may believe" (John 11:11–15).

Jesus did not go immediately because he knew that death was not death and he wanted his followers to know this too.

Notice that in this interchange with the disciples we once

INTERWEAVING OF ALLEGORICAL SIGNS AND SOME RELATED DIALOGUES IN JOHN'S GOSPEL

2:1–12	First Sign—Wedding at Cana
3:1–21	Dialogue with Nicodemus about being "born" again
4:5–26	Dialogue with woman at the well about living "water"
4:27–38	Dialogue with disciples about Jesus' "food"
4:43–54	Second Sign—Cure of Nobleman's Son
5:1–9	Third Sign—Cure of Man at Pool of Bethzatha
5:19–47	Dialogue with Jews about Jesus as judge
6:1–15	Fourth Sign—Miracle of the Loaves
6:16–21	Fifth Sign—Jesus Walks on Water
6:26–40	Dialogue with crowd about Jesus as the "bread" of life
6:41–66	Dialogue with Jews about Jesus as the "bread" of life
7:12	Dialogue with people about Jesus as the "light" of the world
9:1–7	Sixth Sign—Cure of the Man Born Blind
9:4–5, 13–41	Dialogues about Jesus as "light" and spiritual "blindness"
11:1–44	Seventh Sign—Raising of Lazarus
11:21–27	Dialogue with Martha about eternal life

Preceded by a Liturgical Hymn (1:1–18)

Followed by an account of the preparation for the passion (12:1–17:26), the passion itself (18:1–19:42), and the resurrection (20:1–21:25)

---

more hear Jesus speak metaphorically and be understood literally. The misunderstanding gives Jesus (and John) the opportunity to elaborate. When Jesus said "asleep," he meant "dead." However, death is not death, and Jesus wants the opportunity to make this clear.

ALLEGORICAL SIGNIFICANCE OF THE SEVEN SIGNS IN JOHN'S GOSPEL

Sign—material world

1. Water changed to wine at Cana
2. Cure of nobleman's son
3. Cure of man at pool in Bethzatha
4. Miracle of the loaves
5. Jesus walks on water
6. Cure of the man born blind
7. Raising of Lazarus

Significance—spiritual world

At baptism we become a new creation.
We must have faith to grow in Christ.
The risen Christ, through his church, still has power to forgive sins.
The eucharist, Jesus' body and blood, gives spiritual nourishment.
The risen Christ is always with us.
Christ is our light—he reveals the truth and shows us the way to the Father.
Our rebirth in baptism and life in Christ lead to eternal life.

A little further on in his dialogue with Martha, Jesus explains the allegorical meaning of the mighty sign which he will perform when he says, "I am the resurrection and the life; he who believes in me, though he dies, yet shall he live, and whoever lives and believes in me shall never die" (John 11:25–26). John tells the story of the raising of Lazarus to teach his audience that they need not fear death. All who live in the light of Christ will have eternal life.

This is the seventh and last of the mighty signs which John includes in his gospel. In hindsight we can see that the signs describe one's spiritual journey not from birth to death but from birth to eternal life. The seven signs speak of the entire journey: We start with new birth in baptism (wedding feast at Cana). Then we see the necessity for faith rather than for physical proximity (cure of the nobleman's son). We move on to the facts that the risen Christ can still forgive sin (cure at the Sheep Pool), that the risen Christ still nourishes his people (multiplication of the loaves), and that the risen Christ is always with his people (walking on water). We see that we need only keep our eyes on Christ, who is the light of the world (cure of the blind man), in order to reach eternal life (raising of Lazarus).

The purpose of John's signs, then, is to encourage his audience that rather than long for past times when Jesus was physically present, or long for a future time when Jesus will return, they should understand that Christ is present and powerful in their lives right now. They are not separated from Christ. Rather, they will find Christ in his people, in his church, and in his sacraments. John's message to his audience is certainly one which applies to us. For a Christian the good news is that Christ is risen and is alive, present, and powerful right now in the lives of his people.

Review Questions

1. How does the author highlight the question, "Why didn't Jesus go to Lazarus immediately?"
2. What answer to this question did Jesus give his disciples?

THE EFFECT OF JOHN'S ALLEGORICAL METHOD

I. The material world becomes a sign of Christ's presence.

water
bread
light
wine
health (absence of sickness)
life
food

} All symbolize Christ's presence

"All that came to be had life in him" (John 1:1).

II. Everyday experiences become signs of Christ's presence.

Thirst symbolizes longing for Christ.
Hunger symbolizes longing for Christ.
Love reflects the presence of Christ.
Words remind one of the Christ who reveals the Father.
Freedom reminds one of the effects of Christ's passion.
Safety reminds one of Jesus' care.
Fruitfulness reflects union with Christ.

III. Conclusion: Don't look just to history to find Christ. Look to your present experience.

"Now we no longer believe because of what you told us; we have heard him ourselves and we know that he really is the Savior of the world" (John 4:42).

3. What is John teaching his audience through this seventh mighty sign?
4. What is the purpose of John's signs, taken as a whole?

Discussion Questions

1. Do you have any questions about the seven signs and the way they speak allegorically of one's faith journey? What are they?
2. Do you think death is death? Why or why not?
3. In what ways would a belief that we continue to live after "death" affect the way we live now? Explain.

ARTICLE 16

The Washing of the Feet

Question: "Why no institution of the eucharist at the last supper? Why the washing of the feet instead?" (John 13:1–16; John 15:12–15; John 19:41 also discussed)

Not only are the events that take place at "the last supper" different in John than in the synoptics, but, as was noted before, the timing of Jesus' last meal with his disciples is different. As he introduces this last meal the author of John says, "Now before the festival of the passover when Jesus knew that his hour had come to depart out of this world to the Father, having loved his own who were in the world he loved them to the end" (John 13:1). With this sentence John sets both the timing and the tone of Jesus' last meal with his disciples.

As we already know, John pictures Jesus as dying at the same time that the lambs were being slain in preparation for the passover celebration. John makes this clear as Jesus is buried by remarking, "So because of the Jewish day of preparation as the tomb was so close at hand, they laid Jesus there" (John 19:41). John does this to say, allegorically, that Jesus is the Lamb of God whose blood gives life. The Jewish passover celebration has been replaced.

It is true that John does not use the occasion of Jesus' last meal with his disciples to speak of the institution of the eucharist. John has already dealt thoroughly with this theme in chapter 6, with the multiplication of the loaves and the long discourse on Jesus as the bread of life.

Instead of devoting Jesus' last meal with his disciples to the institution of the eucharist, John devotes it to the ramifications of the eucharist. If one joins oneself to Christ, if one becomes one with Christ, what does this mean? What will be expected of those united to Christ?

As always in John, actions have more than one level of meaning. What is Jesus teaching as he washes his disciples' feet?

One obvious meaning is that just as Jesus is willing to act as servant to his disciples, so must they be willing to act as servant to each other. No task done in love for another is menial. Those who are united to Christ love and serve one another.

A second significance of the washing of the feet is evident when one considers the fact that it was customary among the Jews for a student to wash his teacher's feet, not as a servile act but as an act of love and esteem. The disciples think of Jesus as teacher. Jesus acknowledges this when he says, "You call me Teacher and Lord, and you are right, for so I am. If then I, your Lord and Teacher, have washed your feet, you also ought to wash one another's feet" (John 13:13–14).

By washing the disciples' feet Jesus put them in the role of teacher, in the role of those who are loved and esteemed. While they will be assuming this role, they must remember to wash one another's feet.

Still another level of meaning in this incident revolves around the fact that water is an obvious symbol of baptism. It is in this context that Jesus' words to Peter seem most understandable. Jesus says, " 'If I do not wash you, you have no part in me.' Simon Peter said to him, 'Lord, not my feet only but also my hands and my head!' Jesus said to him, 'He who has bathed does not need to wash, except for his feet, but he is clean all over, and you are clean, but not every one of you' " (John 13:8–10).

The word "bathe" was used by the early Christians to refer to baptism. By baptism one does have a part in Christ; one becomes united with Christ. Baptism, unlike the Jewish purification rites, need not be repeated. Once one is "bathed" one is clean all over.

Commentators debate why the words, "except for his feet," are added. Some translations omit this phrase. One possible interpretation is that Jesus, by saying "except for his feet," is alluding to the fact that his disciples will be sent out to serve. In English the phrase "get your hands dirty" carries the same connotation.

Keeping all of these meanings in mind, one can see that Jesus is preparing his disciples for their role after he departs. He is teaching his disciples that they must never lord it over others even though they will be the teachers. Rather they must love and serve each other as equals.

To emphasize the kind of relationships which should exist among his followers Jesus uses the image of loving friends. "This is my commandment, that you love one another as I have loved you. Greater love has no man than he lay down his life for his friends. You are my friends if you do what I command you. No longer do I call you servants . . . but I have called you friends" (John 15:12–15).

Thus we see that John's last supper also deals with "the body of Christ." By picturing Jesus washing the feet of his disciples at their last meal together, John is teaching his audience that if they want to be one with Jesus they must love and serve one another as friends. Only if they "wash one another's feet" will they truly be living in union with Christ.

Review Questions

1. How is the timing different in John's account of Jesus' death?
2. Name three allegorical interpretations of the washing of the feet. Explain each.
3. What image does Jesus use to describe the relationship his followers should have with each other? What is the significance of this image?
4. In what way does John's "last supper" deal with "the body of Christ"?

Discussion Questions

1. What does it mean to say, "Instead of devoting Jesus' last meal with his disciples to the institution of the eucharist, John devotes it to the ramifications of the eucharist"?

2. If one wants to be a disciple and belong to the body of Christ, how will one act?
3. Think about the image of "friendship." How does this image differ from the image of "a loving father"? What do you think John is teaching us when he pictures Jesus using this image to describe how his disciples should interact?

ARTICLE 17

The Role of the Spirit

Question: "How could anyone perform greater works than Jesus?" (John 14:12; John 14:13; 14:16–17; 14:26; 15:25–26; 16:8–11; 16:14–15; Mark 1:10–12 also discussed)

It is during Jesus' farewell discourse to his apostles at the last supper that Jesus says, "Truly, truly, I say to you, he who believes in me will also do the works that I do; and greater works than these will he do, because I go to the Father" (John 14:12).

When Jesus says that his followers will do even greater works than he "because he goes to the Father," he means that the condition for these greater works is his glorification and his sending of the Spirit.

So in order to understand how Jesus' followers could perform "greater works" than Jesus we need to understand the role of the Spirit as it appears in John's gospel.

In this farewell discourse of Jesus, John gives us a more developed theology of the role of the Spirit than we had in the synoptic gospels. In the synoptics the Spirit's role seemed to be to direct Jesus' ministry. At Jesus' baptism the Spirit descended on Jesus and then drove him into the wilderness (see Mark 1:10–12). In John the Spirit's role is to continue Jesus' ministry after Jesus' glorification and until the end of time.

Jesus describes the Spirit with words such as "Counselor" (or "Paraclete" in some translations—John 14:16), as the "Spirit of Truth," (John 14:17), and as the one who "will teach you all things and bring to your remembrance all that I have said to you" (John 14:26).

By looking carefully at these descriptions of the role of the

Spirit we will be able to understand what Jesus meant when he said that his followers would do "greater works" than he.

The word "Counselor" or "Paraclete" is a legal term which means "advocate" or "helper." Only Johannine writings use this word to describe the role of the Spirit. What does John mean by the word?

In John's gospel the Spirit will act as an "advocate" in that the Spirit will take Jesus' side, will defend Jesus in the face of the world's condemnation of him. Jesus explains this to his disciples when he says, " 'They hated me without a cause,' But when the Counselor comes ... he will bear witness to me" (John 15:25–26).

This juridical role is described again when Jesus says, "And when he (the Paraclete) comes, he will convince the world concerning sin and righteousness and judgment. Concerning sin, because they do not believe in me, concerning righteousness, because I go to the Father ... concerning judgment, because the ruler of this world is judged" (John 16:8–11).

The Paraclete will also act as a "helper." The disciples will be left behind in a hostile world but they will not be left orphans. Jesus will send them "another Counselor" who will be with them as he has been with them. "And I will pray the Father, and he will give you another Counselor to be with you forever, even the Spirit of Truth. . . . You know him for he dwells with you and will be in you" (John 14:16–17).

This Counselor is "the Spirit of Truth" not because he reveals a new truth but because he makes the truth already revealed in Christ understandable. As Jesus says, the Spirit will glorify Jesus because "he will take what is mine and declare it to you. All that the Father has is mine; therefore I said that he (the Spirit) will take what is mine and declare it to you" (John 16:14–15).

In Jesus' farewell discourse John is once more teaching his audience that instead of looking for Jesus in the past or in the future they should realize that through the indwelling of the Spirit they are already united with Christ and the Father. The Spirit has become the way to the truth and life of Christ and the Father.

Because Jesus' followers will live in the Spirit they will be able to do "greater works" than did the historical Jesus. Of course these greater works are still Jesus' because they are done in Jesus' name. "Whatever you ask in my name, I will do it" (John 14:13).

What are these works and in what way are they greater? The works themselves are the continuation of Jesus' ministry of teaching and healing, of revealing the Father's love and gathering the flock. Perhaps Jesus was describing these works as greater than his in the sense of geographically greater or numerically greater. For through the Spirit, who enlightens Jesus' followers, the church will extend the words and actions of the historical Jesus to the ends of the earth and to the end of time.

Review Questions

1. What does Jesus' "going to the Father" have to do with people doing "greater works"?
2. What is the role of the Spirit in the synoptics? In John?
3. What does "Counselor" or "Paraclete" mean?
4. How will the Spirit act as an advocate?
5. How will the Spirit act as a helper?
6. Why is the Spirit the "Spirit of Truth"?

Discussion Questions

1. How would you describe the role of the Spirit in the world today?
2. Do you think that the Spirit dwells in you? Why or why not?
3. The Roman Catholic Church accepts both scripture and tradition as revelation. Do you think the role of the Spirit as revealed in John's gospel supports that belief? Why or why not?

ARTICLE 18

The "World" in John's Gospel

Question: "Why does Jesus say he is not praying for the world? I thought God loved the world, and that's why Jesus came." (John 17:9; John 3:16–17; 6:33; 12:47; 13:34–35; 15:10; 15:18–19; 15:22–24; 17:20 also discussed)

The problem behind this question is the meaning of the word "world." John's gospel uses the word with a variety of meanings, very different from each other.

To express God's love for his people as God's love for the "world" is to quote John's gospel. "For God so loved the world that he gave his only Son, that whoever believes in him should not perish but have eternal life. For God sent the Son into the world, not to condemn the world, but that the world might be saved through him" (John 3:16–17).

In this passage the word "world" is used to refer to God's people whom he loves. The same meaning is present when Jesus says, "For the bread of God is that which comes down from heaven and gives life to the world" (John 6:33), and when Jesus says, "For I did not come to judge the world but to save the world" (John 12:47).

In other places in John's gospel, especially in chapters 15 and 16, the word "world" is used in a very different sense. Here "world" refers to all that is in opposition to Christ.

In his farewell discourse Jesus' command to his disciples is love. "As the Father has loved me, so have I loved you. Abide in my love. If you keep my commandments, you will abide in my love, just as I have kept my Father's commandments and abide in his love" (John 15:10).

252

As we saw when discussing the washing of the feet, Jesus taught his disciples a "new commandment": "A new commandment I give to you, that you love one another; even as I have loved you, that you also love one another. By this all men will know that you are my disciples, if you have love for one another" (John 13:34–35).

While the characteristic of the disciples must be love, the characteristic of "the world" is hate. "If the world hates you, know that it has hated me before it hated you. If you were of the world, the world would love its own; but because you are not of the world, but I chose you out of the world, therefore the world hates you" (John 15:18–19).

In this passage we can clearly hear John addressing his contemporaries about the terrible persecution, even unto death, which they face. John's audience knows exactly what it means to be hated by the "world."

Through Jesus' words, John condemns those who hate and persecute Christians. "If I had not come and spoken to them, they would not have sin; but now they have no excuse for their sin. He who hates me hates my Father also. If I had not done among them the works which no one else did, they would not have sin; but now they have seen and hated both me and my Father" (John 15:22–24).

"The world," like "the Jews," has become an expression used to refer to all who have made themselves enemies of Christ and his end of the century disciples, John's audience.

By having Jesus say, "I am praying for them; I am not praying for the world but for those whom thou hast given me" (John 17:9), John is not saying that Jesus no longer loves the world but that this farewell prayer is specifically for these disciples who have known and loved Jesus. Jesus prays that they may be one with the Father, that they may have Christ's joy, and that they may be protected from the evil one as they proclaim the truth in Jesus' name.

Jesus' prayer for his disciples is undoubtedly John's prayer for his contemporaries. In fact John extends the prayer to his own contemporaries, to the church, as he pictures Jesus adding, "I do not pray for these only, but also for those who believe in me through their word" (John 17:20).

Jesus' and John's prayer is that all may be one in the love of the Father, of Jesus, and of the Spirit, so that "the world" may believe (John 17:21).

Review Questions

1. What are two meanings of the word "world" in John's gospel?
2. What is Jesus' command to his disciples as he leaves them?
3. What is the characteristic of the "world" that is in opposition to Christ?
4. In what way are Jesus' words about "the world" speaking directly to the experience of John's audience?
5. Why are the persecutors to blame for their actions?
6. Does Jesus no longer love "the world"? Explain.
7. When Jesus prays for his disciples, for what does he pray?
8. What is John's prayer for his contemporaries?

Discussion Questions

1. Do you think there is anyone in the world on whom Jesus has given up? Why or why not?
2. Do you think Christians today exhibit the kind of love which should identify them as Christ's disciples?
3. Do you think that Jesus' prayer that all his followers are one speaks to the question of unity among various Christian denominations? How?

The Crucifixion:
Jesus' Glorification

Question: "Why did those who came to arrest Jesus fall to the ground when Jesus said, "I am he"? (John 18:6)

As we have noted before, when Jesus says "I am he," he is saying the words which, in Greek, identified Yahweh. That those who came to arrest Jesus "drew back and fell to the ground" on hearing these words is one of many details in John's account of Jesus' passion and death which emphasizes Jesus' divinity.

The "I am" statements in John's gospel are pervasive. In addition to hearing Jesus identify himself with Yahweh by saying "I am he" (John 4:26; 6:20; 8:58), we have seen Jesus identify himself with all that gives life. Jesus has said, "I am the way, the truth and the life" (John 14:6), "I am the bread of life" (John 6:35, 48), "I am the light of the world" (8:12; 9:5), and "I am the resurrection and the life" (John 11:25). As one hears all these statements one realizes that John wants his audience to understand Christ's pervasive presence in everything that is life and gives life. These sayings all remind one of the prologue which says, "All things were made through him, and without him was not anything made that was made. In him was life, and the life was the light of men" (John 1:2-4). In John's gospel all that exists becomes a sign of Christ's loving presence.

In addition to these "I am" statements, we have seen Jesus use some additional metaphors to describe his relationship to his Father and to his disciples. "I am the gate of the sheepfold" (John 10:7), "I am the good shepherd" (John 10:11), and "I am the vine" (John 15:5). Through these metaphors John teaches that Jesus is the way to the Father, that he loves and watches over his disciples, and that he is the source of all their fruitfulness.

Having emphasized Jesus' divinity so consistently throughout his gospel, John does not hesitate to continue this emphasis throughout his account of the passion and death. The emphasis results in quite a different picture than we had in any of the synoptic gospels. In John's passion narrative Jesus always appears in charge.

John has no scene comparable to the agony in the garden. Far from praying to be relieved of his suffering, Jesus seems anxious to embrace it. After Peter strikes the high priest's ear Jesus says to Peter, "Put your sword into its sheath; shall I not drink the cup which the Father has given me?" (John 18:11).

Neither does John have a Simon of Cyrene. Jesus does not need help to carry his cross. Nor does Jesus seem to experience the abandonment which we saw in Mark. John and Mary are at the cross with Jesus.

In addition, we know that Jesus' Father is always with him. Jesus said that this would be so when he warned the disciples of the coming events. "The hour is coming, indeed it has come, when you will be scattered, every man to his home, and will leave me alone. Yet I am not alone, for the Father is with me" (John 16:32).

Jesus dies not as a victim but as one who has completed his work. His last words do not show distress but accomplishment. "It is finished" (John 19:30).

In John's gospel Jesus' death on the cross is not a defeat but a victory. That this would be true has been evident every time the crucifixion has been mentioned. When Jesus spoke of his impending crucifixion he said, "The hour has come for the Son of Man to be glorified" (John 12:23), and "I, when I am lifted up from the earth, will draw all men to myself" (John 12:32).

Jesus also said that when he is crucified people will come to recognize who he is. "When you have lifted up the Son of Man, then you will know that I am he, and that I do nothing on my own authority but speak thus as the Father taught me" (John 8:28).

In John's gospel, then, Jesus' divinity is constantly evident, and never more so than during the passion and death. For John, Jesus' crucifixion is Jesus' glorification, for it is at this time that Jesus has accomplished his Father's will and that Jesus' identity is evident.

Review Questions

1. What claim is embedded in the "I am" statements?
2. What is taught through the metaphor of "gate," "good shepherd," and "vine"?
3. How does John's account of the passion differ from that in the synoptics? Give at least four specific examples.
4. What words does John show Jesus using to refer to the crucifixion?

Discussion Questions

1. When you read of the passion, do you find yourself more attached to the account in one of the synoptics or to John? Why?
2. Which account, the synoptics' or John's, do you think is closer to Jesus' experience? Why?
3. In what way was Jesus' crucifixion his glorification?
4. In the course of stressing Jesus' divinity, does John allow you to see Jesus' humanity? Why or why not?

ARTICLE 20

Blood and Water:
The Birth of the Church

Question: "Why did blood and water come out of Jesus' side? You will probably say, 'Look for an allegorical significance,' but the author seems to make a big point about its being true." (John 19:33–36; John 19:26–27; 7:37–39; 14:16–17; 16:7 also discussed)

As is usual with John's gospel, there is more than one level of meaning to this event.

The most obvious meaning is, of course, that Jesus really did die. Since John has emphasized Jesus' divinity so consistently, one might ask whether Jesus really was human. There is no doubt. Jesus was human and he did die.

A second meaning of this episode is to emphasize a point which we have already discussed. Jesus is the new paschal lamb. Like the lamb of Passover, no bone of Jesus' body is broken. Instead, his side is pierced.

An additional significance may be that Jesus is a sacrificial victim. In Jewish law the blood of sacrificial victims was drained out.

One cannot but note, however, that water and blood are symbols of baptism and the eucharist. We see here an allusion to the water and wine at the first mighty sign at Cana. Water and wine (blood) are symbols of the church's sacraments of initiation. With Christ's death the church is born.

This interpretation is bolstered by the fact that there is a second allusion to the wedding feast at Cana as Jesus dies on the cross, and it too has to do with the birth of the church. Once more Mary is present, and once more Jesus addresses her as "woman." "When Jesus saw his mother, and the disciple whom he loved standing near, he said to his mother, 'Woman, behold your son!' Then he said to the disciple, 'Behold your mother!' " (John 19:26–27). Mary is the mother of the disciple, the mother of those who will bring Christ's love to the world, the mother of the church.

In addition to symbolizing baptism, the water from Christ's side symbolizes the birth of the church in an additional way since it symbolizes the release of the Spirit. The connection between water and the Spirit was made earlier in chapter 7. "On the last day of the feast, the great day, Jesus stood up and proclaimed, 'If any one thirst, let him come to me and drink. He who believes in me, as the scripture has said, "Out of his heart shall flow rivers of living water.' " Now this he said about the Spirit, which those who believed in him were to receive, for as yet the Spirit had not been given because Jesus was not yet glorified" (John 7:37–39).

We know, of course, that Jesus' glorification was his crucifixion. At the time of his death Jesus "gave up his Spirit" (John 19:30). Out of his side flowed living water, the Spirit.

Jesus had earlier promised the disciples that they would receive the Spirit. "And I will pray the Father, and he will give you another Counselor to be with you forever, even the Spirit of Truth, whom the world cannot receive, because it neither sees him nor knows him; you know him for he dwells with you and will be in you" (John 14:16–17).

However, this Spirit cannot come until Jesus has returned to the Father. "Nevertheless I tell you the truth: it is to your advantage that I go away, for if I do not go away, the Counselor will not come to you; but if I go I will send him to you" (John 16:7). The water flowing from Jesus' side symbolizes this Spirit whom Jesus had promised he would send.

Through the pierced side of Jesus, then, the church is born. John wants his audience, and us, to realize that it is in and through the church that we continue to be in contact with the risen Christ.

Review Questions

1. Give four explanations for blood and water coming out of Jesus' side.
2. What allegorical significance is there to Mary's and John's presence at the foot of the cross?
3. What allegorical significance, in addition to baptism, does water have?
4. What is the main teaching, on the allegorical level, of blood and water flowing from Jesus' side?

Discussion Questions

1. In what ways might Mary be called "the mother of the church"?
2. Why would it be important for John to make it clear that Jesus did die?
3. What relationship is there between the Spirit and the church?
4. Do you think of the Spirit as distinct from the Father and the Son? Explain.

Endnote

You have now read the four canonical gospels in the New Testament, and you have learned to appreciate both their similarities and their differences.

The word "gospel," you remember, means "good news." We have four accounts of this good news. The word "gospel," unlike the word "epistle," does not give a clue as to the kind of writing you will be reading when you read this good news. "Gospel" refers to the content and not the form of each of these little books.

As you have seen, the four gospels are not all the same kind of writing. You do not enter a world of historical writing, of biographical writing, or of journalistic writing when you enter the world of any of the gospels. You enter a world of good news that cannot be contained within those parameters because it is a good news that transcends life on earth, a good news that transcends time, a good news that ultimately reaches out and draws the reader into the action.

Each of the gospels steps outside the parameters of historical writing when it assumes the perspective of exploring historical events from a post-resurrection point of view. Each of the gospel authors strives to make these post-resurrection insights not only relevant but central to—all-important to—the lives of each audience.

The good news is that Jesus lives and is at this very instant present and powerful in the lives of his people. Are you facing persecution? Look to Jesus. Are you trying to be faithful to your God, your heritage, your traditions? Look to Jesus. Are you disenfranchised? A pagan? A thief? A person suffering from illness? From poverty? Look to Jesus. Are you isolated, suffering from a sense that real opportunity has passed you by? Do you wonder what this life on earth is actually about, or where one finds the strength and wisdom to live it out with meaning and hope? Look to Jesus. That is the message of each gospel, presented in different ways, formed to meet the needs of each audience. But in the final analysis each is "gospel," each is presenting the good news that Jesus lives. Because Jesus lives, we live. Our lives, our loves find their beginning and end in him. When we begin to understand this good news we have begun to understand the gospels according to Mark, Matthew, Luke and John.

Glossary

Abraham: The first historical person in Jewish salvation history. Abraham lived around 1850 B.C. and is called the father in faith.

Ahaz: King of Judah (the southern kingdom) from 735 to 715 B.C. during the time when Isaiah was a prophet. Ahaz was considered a bad king because he relied on the Assyrians for political protection rather than on God.

Allegory: The name of a literary form (a kind of writing). An allegory has two levels of meaning: a literal level and an intentional level. To understand the author's intent one must figure out what the literal or surface level "stands for." The real topic is on the intentional level.

Alms: To give alms is to give to the poor. To give alms was a social and religious duty for the Jews.

Ambiguity: The quality or state of being ambiguous. A statement is ambiguous if it lends itself to more than one interpretation.

Analogy: A correspondence between two things. Often an analogy is used as part of an explanation—something unknown is compared to something similar which is already known.

263

Angel: The word "angel" means "messenger." The word refers to heavenly spirits.

Antioch: Antioch was in Syria and was a province under Roman rule. The Christian community in Antioch was founded by fugitives who fled from religious persecution in Jerusalem. Antioch became a major Jewish Christian center and may have been the place in which the gospel according to Matthew was written.

Antiochus Epiphanes: King of Syria from 175 to 164 B.C. His imposition of Hellenism and persecution of the Jews resulted in the insurrection of the Jews led by the Maccabee brothers.

Antisemitic: The word "semitic" refers to a group of languages and people of the Near East. The term "antisemitic" names a prejudice against these people, especially against the Jews.

Apocalyptic: The word "apocalyptic" means "revelation." Apocalyptic literature is a kind of writing which uses code words to give hope to people facing persecution. Its message is that the "end time" (the end of the time of suffering) is near.

Apostle: An apostle is one who is sent forth. Jesus' closest disciples, the twelve, were called apostles.

Appropriate: This verb means to take something and make it your own. To appropriate a story would be to retell an existing story in such a way that you give it your own emphasis.

Atonement: An act of atonement (at-one-ment) is an act which brings about union.

Author: The word "author" when used in relation to the gospels does not have the precise meaning that it might suggest to a modern reader. In the case of the synoptic gospels, no "author" identifies himself. The names traditionally associated with the gospels, based on early attributions, are still used, even though certitude as to authorship is not now possible or essential. The synoptic gospels are not the personal eyewitness accounts of one person but the edited arrangements of the oral and written traditions of the community. The gospel of John is said to be based on the testimony of "the disciple whom Jesus loved" (John 21:20–24), but no name is given. So with John's gospel, too, certitude regarding authorship is not possible or necessary.

Beelzebub: The name of a demon. The Pharisees accuse Jesus of acting in the name of this demon.

Bethlehem: Bethlehem is about five miles south of Jerusalem. David was born in Bethlehem, as was Jesus.

Bible: The word means "a collection of books." The Bible includes the Old Testament and the New Testament.

Birth Narrative: The stories about Jesus' birth which appear in Matthew's and Luke's gospels.

Blasphemy: An act which is contemptuous of God. The Pharisees accuse Jesus of blasphemy because he makes claims which could be true only of God.

Brother: In the Greek New Testament this word has a less precise meaning than it has in English. Jesus' "brothers" could be relatives, close friends, or followers.

Canon: A "canon" is an instrument by which something is measured. In the context of the Bible, the canon refers to the books which are considered revelation and inspired and are therefore in the Bible. These books are the "rule" of faith.

Centurion: A centurion was in charge of one hundred men in the Roman army.

Chief Priests: The heads of priestly families. The priests had special functions: they gave oracles, presented instructions about the law, and offered sacrifice. In New Testament times the priests appear as part of an aristocracy that opposed Jesus.

Christ: The word "christ" means "anointed." The word is a messianic title, applied to those whom the Jews understood to be God's instruments to save them. To apply the word to Jesus is to claim that Jesus is the messiah.

Christology: Centers on Christ. Christology studies Jesus, his nature, and his function.

Church: The word means "the assembly of ones called out." In the New Testament context, "church" refers to the Christian community—those who are united with Jesus Christ.

Coliseum: An amphitheater in Rome in which many Christians died.

Collate: To gather and arrange in a particular order.

Consanguinity: Refers to a blood relationship. A brother and sister could not marry because of the laws of "consanguinity."

Context: That which surrounds a word or passage. The context within which something is said or written affects its meaning.

Contextualist: A person who reads in context. In relation to the Bible, a contextualist would ask: "What is the literary form of this book? What were the beliefs of the people of the time? How does this fit into the process of revelation?"

Covenant: A solemn ritual agreement which could not be broken. The word "covenant" is used to describe the relationship between God and his people.

David: Succeeded Saul as king (ca. 1010–970 B.C.). He united the twelve tribes and defeated the Philistines. David was seen as an ideal ruler. People expected the messiah to be one like David.

Defense Mechanism: This is a psychological term to describe how we defend ourselves in our relationship with others or even with ourselves. Defense mechanisms can be unconscious ways of responding to a perceived threat.

Disciple: A disciple is one who learns from and passes on the teachings of another. Jesus' followers, including his apostles, are referred to as disciples.

Dramatic Irony: Dramatic irony exists when an author or narrator (the voice telling the story) and an audience share information which the characters in a story do not share. Mark's gospel is an example of dramatic irony because the author and audience know that Jesus is the Son of God but the characters in the story, such as Jesus' apostles, do not know this.

Dramatization: The act of turning something into a drama. If one were to dramatize an internal temptation the temptation would be personified—would become a character and would speak.

Ecumenical: Worldwide in its range. An ecumenical council would call together people from all over the world. The ecumenical movement seeks worldwide unity and understanding among religions.

Egypt: The country around the valley of the Nile River, bordering the southeast side of the Mediterranean.

Elders: A member of the council of the elders, so a person of standing in the religious community, along with scribes, priests, and Pharisees.

Emmanuel: The word means "God with us." Isaiah used this word to name the hoped-for infant in Isaiah 7:10–17. Matthew refers to Isaiah's words in his account of the revelation to Joseph (Matthew 1:23).

Ephesus: The capital of the Roman province of Asia, a wealthy port and marketplace. Paul preached in Ephesus on both his second and his third journeys. Ephesus is a possible site for the composition of Luke's and John's gospels.

Eschatology: The word means "study of last things." When Jesus speaks of the end times his words are about "eschatology."

Eucharist: The word means "thanksgiving." It is used to name the communion service initiated by Jesus at the last supper and celebrated by Christians.

Evangelize: To preach the gospel.

Exodus: The core experience in Jewish salvation history when God lead his people out of Egypt and through the desert to the holy land.

Form: The shape of something. In literature the form is the kind of writing, or the "shape" of the whole piece. Is it a poem? a letter? a legend? One cannot understand the author's intent unless one understands the literary form in which the author is writing.

Function: The use to which something is put, or its role. In literature different kinds of writing have different functions. An editorial has a different function than a straight news story or a feature article.

Genealogy: The record of familial descent. In Israelite society a person's rights and privileges depended on his membership in a class or tribe, so genealogies were all-important. Legal paternity conferred all the rights of natural paternity, so the function of a genealogy was not always to trace a blood line.

Gentile: Any non-Jew. A Gentile is a "foreigner" from the point of view of the Jews.

Gerasene Demoniac: Gerasa was a Hellenistic city which Jesus and his followers visited. This city is the setting for the story of the exorcism of "Legion." The person from whom "legion" was exorcised is called the "Gerasene demoniac."

Gospel: The word means "good news." In the context of the New Testament the word refers to the four accounts of the good news—Mark, Matthew, Luke and John.

Gospel According to John: This gospel is thought to have been written to an end of the century audience. The suspected late date causes scholars to question whether the author is John the apostle or John the elder. Was John the apostle martyred with his brother James in 44 A.D., as one tradition holds, or did he live to an old age in Ephesus, as another tradition holds? No definitive answer can be given. The gospel itself does not equate the beloved disciple with the apostle John.

Gospel According to Luke: This gospel is thought to have been written to Gentiles around 85 A.D. The traditional attribution to Luke, the companion of Paul, is not seriously disputed. No clear tradition exists as to location. Scholars suggest Ephesus, a Greek-speaking city in Asia Minor, as a likely setting.

Gospel According to Mark: This gospel is thought to have been written to persecuted Christians around 65 A.D. The gospel is attributed to Mark, who worked with Peter in Rome. Some scholars argue that Syria or Palestine is a more likely setting than Rome.

Gospel According to Matthew: This gospel is thought to have been written to Jewish Christians, quite possibly in Antioch around 80 A.D. The gospel is attributed to Matthew the apostle. However, the attribution rests on a statement of Papias (130 A.D.), quoted by Eusebius, that Matthew composed the discourses of Jesus in Aramaic. Since scholars do not think that our Greek "gospel according to Matthew" is a translation of these Aramaic discourses, scholars doubt the attribution to Matthew.

Greek Koine: The common Greek in which the New Testament was originally written. It was the Greek of the marketplace rather than classical Greek.

Hebrew: This word is used to name the Israelites, especially in their relationships with "foreigners."

Hebrew Language: The language in which the Old Testament was written.

Hellenism: The influence of the Greek culture on the eastern Mediterranean world which began with Alexander the Great (356–323) but continued long after his death.

Herod: Herod is the name of seven Palestinian rulers. Herod I, known as Herod the Great, was king of Judea when Jesus was born. Herod Antipas, the son of Herod the Great, was tetrarch of Galilee and Perea at the time Jesus was crucified. He executed John the Baptist and presided at Jesus' trial.

Historical: An event is historical if it was witnessed and if we have oral or written accounts of the event. Not all events are historical. Some precede history. Others transcend history. To say that an event is not historical is not necessarily to deny that it happened.

Hyperbole: Exaggeration.

Hypocrite: A person who lacks sincerity, who says one thing and does another.

Image: A mental conceptualization of something not present to the senses. A concrete way of thinking about an abstract concept.

Immanuel: See Emmanuel.

Infancy Narrative: See Birth Narrative.

Inspiration: The state of being affected by divine influence. When we say that the Bible is inspired we mean that God affected the human authors.

Irony: A tone used so that the literal meaning of words is different than the intentional meaning, sometimes even opposite.

Isaiah: The prophet who lived at the time of Ahaz (734–715 B.C.).

Isaiah: The name of a prophetic book of the Bible which contains the work of three prophets from three historical periods.

Jesus: The name means "Yahweh is salvation." The word "Jesus" is used by scholars to refer to the historical person as distinct from the risen Christ.

Jew: Used to name the Israelites in both an ethnic and a religious sense.

John: One of the apostles—a son of Zebedee and brother of James. The authorship of the gospel according to John is attributed to him. See "Gospel According to John."

John the Baptist: The son of Zechariah and Elizabeth; the cousin of Jesus who baptized Jesus.

John the Elder: Some scholars think that John the elder was the beloved disciple who wrote the gospel according to John. If so, this John may have been a very young eyewitness to events in

Jerusalem and an old and wise mystic living in Ephesus in 90 A.D.

Joseph: A patriarch who was sold by his brothers, rose to high office in Egypt, and then saved his family by providing them with food during the famine.

Joseph: Mary's husband. Jesus' stepfather.

Judas Iscariot: The apostle who betrayed Jesus.

Koine: See Greek Koine.

"L": Material found only in Luke's Gospel. "L" is probably not a single source.

Leaven: A substance like yeast which was used in making bread.

Legalist: A person who obeys the letter of the law but misses the spirit of the law. The Pharisees are depicted as legalists.

Legend: An imaginative and symbolic story with an historical core.

Legion: The largest division of the Roman armies. The word "legion" is used to mean "many" when applied to either demons (Mark 5:9) or angels (Matthew 26:53).

Leper: A person who suffered from the disease of leprosy. Such a person was an outcast of society.

Lintel: The horizontal beam on the upper part of a window or door.

Literary Form: The kind of writing. Examples are poetry, fable, myth, history, biography, science fiction, etc. In order to understand any book you need to know its literary form.

Literary Technique: A systematic way of accomplishing something in a written work. Luke uses a trip as a literary technique around which to organize his gospel. John uses "signs" and dialogue/monologues as a literary technique to probe mystery.

Luke: A companion and fellow worker of Paul's. The authorship of the gospel according to Luke is attributed to him. See "Gospel According to Luke."

"M": Material found only in Matthew's gospel. "M" is probably not a single source.

Mark (also called John Mark): A Jerusalem Jew who traveled with Barnabas and Paul on the first journey before Paul and Mark had a falling out. Mark is thought to have worked with Peter in Rome. The gospel according to Mark is attributed to him. See "Gospel According to Mark."

Matthew: One of the apostles, a Jewish tax collector. The gospel according to Matthew is attributed to him but scholars dispute this attribution. See "Gospel According to Matthew."

Messiah: Hebrew for "anointed one." "Messiah" and "Christ" are synonyms. Both are used to identify Jesus as God's saving instrument.

Messianic Title: A title which names Jesus as the expected Messiah, i.e. "Christ," "Son of David," "Son of Man."

Metaphor: A metaphor is a comparison that does not use "like" or "as." A comparison which does use "like" or "as" is a simile. Example: Simile—The nurse is like an angel. Metaphor—The nurse is an angel.

Miracle Story: A story which reveals God's saving power. It usually includes: an introduction that presents the situation; a request for help; an account of help given; the result of the help; the reaction of the spectators.

Narrative: The act, technique, or way of telling a story.

Narrator: The "voice" telling the story. The narrator cannot always be equated with the author. The author may create a character who tells the story and is thus the narrative voice.

Nazareth: Nazareth is located in lower Galilee. Jesus spent his youth in Nazareth.

Nicodemus: The Jewish leader who came to Jesus by night (John 3:1ff). He later defended Jesus (John 7:50) and helped bury Jesus.

Oral Tradition: The traditions of the community handed on by word of mouth.

Pagan: A person who has no religion, or who is neither Christian, Moslem, nor Jewish.

Palestine: The strip of land bordering the eastern side of the Mediterranean Sea.

Parable: A parable is a story which, at base, rests on a metaphor. The comparison is between the audience and the story itself. The function of the parable is to correct and call to conversion the audience.

Paradox: A paradox exists when two facts are both true but they appear to contradict each other. Example: The kingdom of God is "now." The kingdom of God is "not yet."

Passover: The Jewish festival that celebrates the escape of the Jews from Egypt.

Pastoral: A pastoral response is one which is shaped to meet the needs of the audience or "flock." A "pastor" is a "shepherd."

One image of Jesus is that of the good shepherd. Jesus' sensitivity to sinners is an example of a pastoral rather than a judgmental response.

Personification: Describing inanimate objects or abstract ideas with human characteristics. A snake talking is an example of personification.

Pharisees: Members of a leading religious sect in Judaism that stressed scrupulous observance of the law. In the synoptic gospels most Pharisees oppose Jesus.

Pilate: Pilate is also called Pontius Pilate. He was the Roman prefect of Judea at the time of Jesus' trial and sentenced him to be crucified.

Proof Texting: To misuse biblical passages by taking them out of context and using them to "prove" the truth of statements which the biblical passages are not addressing.

Prophet: One who speaks for another. In the context of scripture, one who speaks for God and who constantly reminds the people of the ramifications of living in covenant love.

"Q": The first letter of the German word for source. "Q" names the collection of sayings found in both Matthew's and Luke's gospels and is thought to be a common source.

Revelation: That which makes known God's will and truth. When we claim that the Bible is revelation we claim that it reveals the truth about God, our relationship with God, and what we should be doing to build up rather than tear down the kingdom.

Roman Empire: All of the events which we read about in the gospels, as well as the social settings in which the four gospels were written, occur against the backdrop of the imperial power of Rome. Palestine became a Roman province in 63 B.C. and remained so through all of New Testament times.

Sadducees: A Jewish sect. They were extremely conservative aristocrats who accepted only the torah. Their disagreements with the Pharisees included the fact that they did not believe in the resurrection.

Samaritans: Residents of Samaria. The Jews considered the Samaritans an heretical group and detested them.

Satan: The evil one who tempts Jesus. Although Satan is strong and causes much evil, he is not stronger than God.

Scribes: The scribes were members of the aristocracy in that they were the intellectuals in their society. The scribes were experts on the law. Most scribes belonged to the Pharisee sect.

Septuagint: The Greek translation of the Old Testament begun around 250 B.C.

Simon: Simon was the Pharisee to whom Jesus told the parable of the two debtors.

Simon Peter: Simon Peter is more often called Peter. He is the apostle who denies Jesus but later becomes the apostolic leader.

Socratic Irony: A technique used by good teachers. A question is asked not because the teacher doesn't know the answer but because the teacher wants to challenge and spur on the thinking of the student. The question often appears to be simple-minded and off the subject.

Son of Man: A messianic title which Jesus is pictured as applying to himself. The "Son of Man" is a "great and glorious king" title from the book of Daniel, but Jesus links the "Son of Man" with suffering.

Synagogue: The word means "assembly" or "collection." After the destruction of the temple in 587 B.C. synagogues arose.

The synagogue was a meeting house for prayer and study of the law rather than a place for sacrifice.

Synonym: A word which has the same meaning as another word.

Synoptic Gospels: Mark's, Matthew's, and Luke's gospels are the synoptic gospels because they have many similarities and can be seen as one.

Temple: The temple in Jerusalem was the only authorized center for sacrifice and for the worship of Yahweh. The first temple was destroyed in 587 B.C. The temple which existed during Jesus' life was destroyed in 70 A.D.

Testament, New: "Testament" means "covenant." The New Testament is the collection of Christian Greek scriptures.

Testament, Old: "Testament" means "covenant." The Old Testament is the collection of Jewish Hebrew scriptures.

Theme: The main idea or perception expanded upon in a larger work.

Theology: The study of God.

Tithe: A tithe was a tenth of one's income which was to be given to the support of others—usually to support a government or religion.

Tone: The pitch of a word which determines its meaning or the general effect or atmosphere created.

Vocation: One's call—one's life's work.

Webb, Jack: A character in the TV program "Dragnet" who was a police detective and always wanted "just the facts."

Yahweh: A translation of the name of God as revealed to Moses. Many scholars believe that the name is derived from the Hebrew verb "to be" and means "He is."

Index of Biblical References

278